REFLECTIONS OF A CAREGIVER

FAITH
— IN MY —
CORNER
No One Fights Alone

LISA F. HARRIS

IMPORTANT NOTE

This book has been written based on the authors' personal experiences, knowledge, and opinions. The topics and personal research expressed by the author are not to diagnose or prescribe in any manner to any physical ailments. Please consult with your physician.

FAITH IN MY CORNER NO ONE FIGHTS ALONE
Reflections of a Caregiver

Lisa F. Harris
Ladylisaharris@gmail.com

ISBN 978-1-949826-40-1
Printed in the USA.
All rights reserved

Make Up Artist (Author back cover Photo) : Beatrice Flowers
IG: theebeautybea

Photoghapher (Author photos): Raynard Graves
IG: headshotboutique

Published by: EAGLES GLOBAL BOOKS | Frisco, Texas
In conjunction with the 2021 Eagles Authors Course
Cover & interior designed by DestinedToPublish.com

My God

With sincerity, I appreciate Abba Father for HIS faithfulness, grace, mercy, and strength. When I am weak, He is strong. We would not have survived the rounds without HIM.

DEDICATION

My Best Friend

To my life, my love, my number one fan, Eriq: Thank you for allowing me to care for you and to share your story and my reflections as your caregiver so that others can see how important it is that when God has called someone to care for another, they must focus on Elohim and themselves along the way in order to fulfill their assignment as a caregiver. I thank you for your support, your sacrifice, and the encouragement you have given me to complete this manuscript. I love you, and just like our wedding vow said, "Can two walk together except they agree?" I still agree, and I could never have done this without you! Love you, babe.

I dedicate this book to my children, Brittany, Eriq Jr., Emanuel, Faith, and Elijah. I love God and thank Him for you all. During the second round of the fight, you guys were not just firsthand spectators but also became caregivers to us both. Continue showing love and support for each other as siblings, and remember, Faith is always in your corner.

And to G-Ma's tribe which adds a loving dimension to my world: Rhianna, Dylan, Giselle, Maszel, and Emoni, delight in the Lord, and honor your mother and father.

To my mom, Eldora Fleming: I love you. You modeled caregiving without saying a word. It was evident in your patience, strength, and unrestricted love when you cared for your dad, brother-in-law, husband (my dad), and others.

To my sister, Sharon: I love you for being there for Mom. With your beautiful heart and gentle nature, you cared for my children with love, transportation, time, and laughter so that I could care for their dad.

To my niece, Tiffany Cogshell: You, too was a caregiver as you checked on Paw-paw. Keep God first!

To my mother in love, Hattie Stuckey: I love you for showing Eriq how to love unconditionally. I appreciate your support, prayers, and meals.

To Derik and Shirley Harris: Take care of mom. Thank you for being there, right in the fight!

To Tondalah (Walter) Stroud: Thank you for over forty years of friendship, reflecting sisterhood as you have lent your heart, support, and time. Much love!

FOREWORD

Faith in My Corner: As I read this book, it brought back many memories of my three victories over cancer and how God gave my beautiful wife of twenty-nine years the Grace to be in my corner as my caregiver. As you read this book, ask God for the grace to handle the physical, emotional, psychological, and spiritual aspects of being a caregiver. This book is a testimony of how Lisa stood on the promises of God. Because she trusted God and stayed in her corner, she was able to see the manifested power of God through her prayers as she gracefully performed the duties of a caregiver. This book will also help you.

Dr. Eric T. Harris, Sr.

Apostle | Temple of Deliverance Life Changing Ministries|
Chicago, Illinois apostleeq55@gmail.com
Author of God's Prescription For Healing

FOREWORD

Faith in my Corner is an inspiring read to encourage the giver and recipient of ***actionable faith***. ***Faith*** is the ***substance*** of things—***words of truth—hoped for/believed,*** the ***evidence*** of things—the ***manifestation of every promise***—that you ***can't see at the time you ask.*** As I read this book from a registered nurse's perspective, I am moved to tears but also strengthened! In my seventeen years as a registered nurse, I have witnessed patients' need for caregiver support. There have been episodes when family members have rejected their loved ones because of the ***weight*** of the care needed as well as caregivers who haven't realized the extent of their ***strength*** or ***responsibility***. Every person with 'breath' will at some point need a caregiver, whether it is for their spouse, child, parent, or friend. *Faith in my Corner* allows us to take a ***proactive*** approach. Pastor "Lady" Lisa has captured the essence of a ***caregiver***, detailing the ***biblical*** character traits needed to become steady and steadfast in a journey we were ***slated*** to overcome! ***No one fights alone . . . The fight is fixed . . . You win!***

Honored by love,

Ambassador Amelia Luckie, RN, BSN
Rophe Healthcare Adult Day Service Center
South Holland, Illinois |www.rophehealthcare.com

FOREWORD

As a caregiver for our special needs son, Terrell, I know firsthand some of the challenges a caregiver experiences. Pastor Lisa's account was both thought-provoking and intriguing. The analogy of an actual fight helped to drive home the points regarding what a caregiver endured. I believe this book will lift and inspire all who read it. The result will be victory!

Honored by love,

Pastor, Lady Gloria Alford

Progressive- Life Giving Word Cathedral
Hillside, Illinois | www.plgwc.org

PREFACE

I was born and raised in the windy city, Chicago. I grew up in a Christian home, and my sister was the oldest. I like to think that, as I was growing up, I was a pretty average well-rounded person who loves the Lord, people, sports, dogs, reading, dance, makeup, fashion, family gatherings, and vacations. While in high school, I spent several summers at the hospital, working in the pre-operative surgical department and later worked as a CNA. I went on to obtain a bachelor's degree in nursing and in religious education. My passion is to inspire, empower, and equip others, which is why I became a holistic health coach and continue in that role to date. According to USLegal.com, a caregiver is someone over the age of 18 who provides care for another, and according to Dictionary.com, a caregiver is a person who cares for someone who is sick or disabled and an adult who cares for an infant or child. Caregiving is not limited to supporting another person who is sick, injured or has a disability. It also consists of direct care, protection, and supervision. Matthew 5:9 tells us, *"Blessed are the peacemakers, for they shall be called children of God."* As a caregiver, you are bringing peace to those in need.

When I set out, I did not know my life journey would take the road that it did. But in the midst of it all, I am grateful. I have been blessed. I found joy with the plans that the Lord had laid out for me. I learned to embrace the detour. I called it a detour because I had no idea that I would encounter life that way, but, again, the word of God reminds me that His thoughts are not my thoughts, yet His grace is sufficient.

The work I was doing was not enough. My works had to be in partnership with my Faith. I had to wholeheartedly know, "God, I cannot handle it, but You can. God, you are the one to do exceedingly and abundantly above all I could ever think or ask." Faith was right there to restore and comfort me.

God showed me that alone, the various works did not produce Faith. It was not until I bridged my works with Faith that all things became possible. Faith and works were married together to yield the promises of God. On every occasion, the word of God gave me the effect of longing. I couldn't have one without the other. I was an ambitious woman who was thoughtful, loving, loyal to God and my family, outgoing, intelligent, trustworthy, and strong—yielding kind submission to others in accordance with Ephesians 5:21, which said, "Submit yourselves one to another in fear of God." More importantly, God loved me. I am a child of the Most High God. One of my favorite scriptures stated, "*It is in him that I live, move, and exist*" (Acts 17:28).

Now, I want to share how I was able to care for a loved one and hold him up. Everyone's story is different. However, all of the stories have a common denominator: love. The person taking care of their loved one may become overwhelmed and may or may not identify with some stress.

What do you do when you experience a moment of being so overwhelmed that you just burst out into tears? How do you keep up your daily routine and activities? How do you remind yourself that you need proper exercise? Do you take a moment and breathe? How do you handle being emotionally, physically, or spiritually depleted at times?

The virtuous woman in the Bible (Proverbs 31) was a multitasker, and so many of us women today can relate to that. However, one can overlook a passage in the story; not only was she a virtuous woman, but she also took time to take care of herself.

Taking time for yourself will give you the strength to continue to do for others. While I believe this is true, it was not as easy as it sounds. On most days, I was filled with joy; there was no way a punch by the enemy would keep me down in this fight.

God has given me the grace to minister in my capacity as a caregiver. My hands are His hands, and, no matter what comes my way, while depending on God, I have learned to dance in the rain even in difficult situations. I am confident that I can contend for the win because no one fights alone. God will never leave me in the midst of a storm that may come my way.

There is a spinoff to caregiving; whether nursing another to health or helping with their aspirations, one must be aware and must learn to take care of themselves. Life is like a roller coaster; you meet many opportunities to learn new things, face challenges, and enjoy all of the wonderful celebratory events, that is, if you embrace them. Enjoy the totality of you! Do not just hold on to your dreams; begin to birth your goals. The time is now!

I quote the wise words of Dr. Martin Luther King, Jr.: "Faith is taking the first step even when you can't see the whole staircase." Caregiver, be kind to yourself, love yourself, and know that there is value in you!

ACKNOWLEDGMENTS

To **TOD, my church family:** I love and appreciate you all. I am ever grateful for the various ways you all have supported us through the years. Whether you called, prayed, visited, sent a card, or provide a meal. Again, I Bless you in Jesus' name. Remember, Faith is in your corner! Hold on to God's unchanging hand.

To **Apostle Donald and Lady Gloria Alford, our spiritual parents:** Thank you for your prayers and for displaying what marriage should reflect in the eyes of the Lord!

Finally, **special thanks to the amazing beta readers, the coaches, and the editors,** who provided their professional and honest feedback during the process : Much love!

SPECIAL THANKS

My heartfelt thanks to two great pillars of our
family that have gone on before me:

The Late Rev. Mosezel Fleming (Dad)

The Late Albert Stuckey (Father-in-law)

.

CONTENTS

INTRODUCTION

OUR BEGINNING

> "Ye shall not need to fight in this battle: set
> yourselves, stand ye still, and see the salvation of
> the Lord with you." (2 Chronicles 20:17)

On August 15, 1992, I said, "I do," to the love of my life. We met while we were both working at a hospital in Chicago in our early twenties. I knew he would be my husband; his loving God first meant that loving me would be in alignment with Ephesians 5:25, which stated, *Husbands, love your wives, even as Christ also loved the church, and gave himself for it.* God was the center of our marriage, so He was the center of our family, and instructions came from above and not from outside.

We had strong love for each other. We enjoyed fifteen years without major concerns regarding our health. And then, in addition to being my husband's best friend, wife, pastor wife and soulmate, I became his spousal caregiver in the summer of 2007.

Nothing could have prepared me for this type of challenge, not even my BSN degree or my having worked in the hospice and medical oncology unit. My husband and I were in a battle for our lives. We were in a fight for our health. Notice that I say, "We were diagnosed." We are one body. When your spouse is diagnosed with cancer not once but thrice, you feel what they feel. Cancer is a real fight. While everyone in the stands, including family, friends, and strangers, was screaming, not all of the advice was good, and not all of it was meant for us both.

The CDC (Center For Disease Control) describes chronic illness as a disease that lasts three months or longer. Whatever your preparation, you are called upon to serve, make decisions, and provide care for your spouse or loved one; immediate on-the-job training begins. From the initial onset of the cancer, everything happened quickly. I was shocked, stunned, and unprepared, or so I thought. But God has a way of bringing out the best in a person! When transitioning to a new way of life, one can quickly feel alone. At times, I was at a loss, not knowing how to express my feelings regarding the sickness. I felt that, out of all people, I should not complain, so I just absorbed my feelings and carried on. I repented when my actions did not line up with the fruit of the spirit that displayed patience. It was the grace of God that kept me.

There were times when I felt family and friends were not being sensitive. I would hear some say, "How is he doing?" in a solemn voice. Alternatively, they would have this look of distress on their faces as they asked me, "Are you okay?" I wasn't okay. At times, I didn't know if some were supporting us in genuine concern about what was going on or they were just curious to see how we were handling the situation. It's important to know that the caregiver story has value. The caregiver's pain is never the same as that of the person who has been diagnosed, but the caregiver feels the squeeze. Even though the caregiver looks physically healthy, they may experience various disturbing and mind-blowing emotions.

The grace of God showed me how to identify and disengage from the negative triggers and struggles that were unfolding. I was angry and frustrated, not at my husband but at the illness. Never wanting to sit on the sidelines and watch from a distance, I chose to be in my marriage 100% and to be hands-on through it all. I would take my husband to every visit and treatment. I made sure that the medical staff addressed all our concerns. I did research on the various stages of cancer and the symptoms he was experiencing while attending classes that taught me how to cook the foods that would strengthen his immune system. We continued to date each other by cuddling at home and watching movies. I even talked to God about all my whiny human feelings: *Why my husband? Why this sickness? Where did it come from? What caused this? What lifestyle changes do we need to make? How did I not see this?*

Having to fulfill the emotional, mental, physical, and spiritual aspects of a caregiver's role is not easy. Having the compassion to care for others is different from having and holding the capacity to be a caregiver. It was and is by the grace of God that I was given the ability to serve, support, and minister to my husband. While the journey did become tiring at times, I was blessed by God that I was able to partake in another aspect of my husband's life. Although we would both have preferred for our lives not to take this detour, God carried us through. My husband would often say to me that he would never have wanted to put me through such an experience. And I would say to him that I would never have wanted him to go through it without me!

The fight was called, and we were in it to win it, and it was for His Glory! Have you ever watched a boxing match? After every round, the bell rings, and the fighters go to their corners. While a fighter is in the corner, a person can come in and approach the fighter—a cornerman or cutman, they call him. His responsibility is to treat any physical harm done to the fighter before and during that fight. The trainer is also vital to the boxer; he helps prepare the fighter mentally, physically, and emotionally for the upcoming battle. While in the fight, the most important person the fighter can listen to is the person in the corner. The job of the man in the corner is to see what the fighter doesn't see and to bring that to the fighter's attention. In a fight, the boxer wants to hear only one voice.

Death and life are in the power of one's tongue (Proverbs 18:21). We should guard our thoughts carefully because life flows from them. In the first round, we were hit with the news of cancer. I would have nightmares of being a widow. For that reason, I had some sleepless nights. I immediately cast out that thought and declared that Eriq would have a long life on this earth. The boxing match had begun. Round one tried to take us out. That first blow was complex, with the diagnosis of the stage and type of cancer and no known family history of the disease.

During the fight, there were multiple jabs of pain, weight loss, and loss of appetite. We sent jabs right back with healthy foods, exercise, and a host of Scriptures. We stood our ground, holding onto the word that no weapon that formed against us would prosper (Isaiah 54:17). The enemy even attempted an illegal hit to the head, trying to attack my mind by saying that I would soon be alone. So, I looked the enemy back in the face and returned the punch with the words "I'm not going out like that." I would remember what my trainer had told me about casting my burdens upon him. During shadowboxing, the trainer had said death and life were in the power of my tongue (Proverbs 18:21). So I begin to speak life into the cancerous cells to eradicate them in Jesus's name!

The bell rang, and back to our corner we went. Now, each round in a fight lasts only about three minutes. I'll be honest with you: That round felt like overtime. We had twelve weeks of treatment. So, I took advantage of the one-minute intervals between the rounds and rested. The Lord tells us to rest in Him. In the midst of the fight, remember the cues from your coach as he shouts, "Who forgiveth all thine iniquities; who health all thy diseases?" (Psalm 103:3). Also remember His words: "My help cometh from the Lord" (Psalm 121) and "I shall not die but live and declare the works of the Lord" (Psalm 118:17).

I watched as the cutman came and repaired my husband's colon by applying both the treatments and surgery and by sealing his wound with the manifestation of healing. In round two, the fight resumed, and the enemy threw a cross punch toward me. When the bell rang, the trainer stepped in and stopped the glowing hot sensitivity within my body. In round three, the enemy gave a lead hook punch to my husband's left lung. Once again, when the bell rang, the cut man was right there and sealed the cut with a healing balm. In round four, the enemy directed a rear hook to my husband's lower back, and, as always, when the bell rang, the cut man came and sealed off the tumor. During the fight, I was rolling with the punches of unknown symptoms in my body that the doctors could not explain. It was not the time to throw in the towel.

If you are in a similar situation, hold your position, stand still, and see the salvation of the Lord; it's not time to tap out. Although it may look like the enemy has the upper hand to those watching you and he may push you up against the rope at times, stay in the fight and hold your ground. All your pain and training are about to pay off. The Scripture tells us to train for godliness because there is a promise to this present life and the life to come (1 Timothy 4:8). Oh, but there was something about the trainer on our side; he came right in when the bell rang and treated the cut on my husband's lower back and turned around and applied his healing to my undiagnosed ailments.

Now, as you may know, in anticipation of the fight, the trainer works with the boxer one-on-one daily, preparing them mentally and physically and bringing discipline into their life. Yes, the boxer trains while experiencing pain, and Hebrews 12:11 (ESV) tells us, "For the moment all discipline seems painful rather than pleasant, but later it yields the peaceful fruit of righteousness to those who have been trained by it." God tells us that man should not live on bread alone but on every word that proceeds out of His mouth (Matthew 4:4). The spiritual training entails memorizing and reading the scriptures and praying daily.

One of the trainer's duties is to keep pushing the fighter in order to make them better. The word of God tells us to study to show ourselves approved unto God, a workman that needeth not to be ashamed, rightly dividing the word of truth. (2 Timothy 2:15), You may be wondering how long you should work out? You should work out daily, pray without ceasing. The Holy Spirit stands and intercedes on our behalf. Knowing this, I can relate to the Scripture that talks about tribulation working patience within us (Romans 5:3). Do you know that it's the trainer who helps determine the outcome? This amazing cutman and trainer in our corner is the Lord God Almighty. The Holy Spirit makes intercession for you! He is the same cutman, cornerman, and trainer. There is always a direct connection to your trainer, and you can quickly call Him and tell Him what you want. This trainer here will always give you clear instructions to follow. He will not tell you anything different from what He has told his other fighters. We are all given the same training manual, and the word of God shows us that His word changes not (Isaiah 40:8). From the manual, you will be able to apply the Scripture for every punch thrown your way. The Lord is awesome; He will even tell you that this battle is not yours and tell you to stand your ground and move at His command. During a fight, remember to listen to the still, small voice of your trainer. In the midst of the crowd's roaring, hear the voice that says, "The just shall live by faith" (Romans 1:17).

Do you want to know who won the fight? We did. We were more than conquerors (Romans 8:37), satan was defeated. Jesus paid the price for your healing. The cornerman tells you who the winner of the fight is initially by saying, "Victory is ours": "And they overcame him by the blood of the Lamb and by the word of their testimony" (Revelation 12:11). I ask you, who is your trainer? Who is your cutman? Who is your cornerman? Three different people or one person can hold these three positions. My cornerman, His name is Jesus Christ! He can see from every angle, knows all the right openings. God cares for your mind, body, and soul; He longs for you to be close to Him! So let your heart take courage in every situation.

Since 2007, I have kept an organized journal of this journey. I encountered writer's block while trying to tell this story on paper when it came to revisiting the various events. It began to feel like it had just begun. I had even put off writing this book after my husband's initial diagnosis of cancer, but, deep in my heart, I felt that it was time to share the fight from the caregiver's point of view. I wanted to talk about how the illness could affect the caregiver and how important it was for the caregiver to be the patient's advocate and to be proactive in their healing process. There is hope. You can fulfil your calling as a caregiver or support person without losing yourself during it all.

I want to encourage you to refill your cup, refresh your mind, body, and soul. Remember that your work will be produced by faith, your labor will be prompted by the love and your strength will be renewed as an eagle; know that your hope and healing is found in Jesus Christ (1 Thessalonians 1:3). Others have gone down this path before you to let you know that you are not alone. The Lord is near to all who will call upon Him, in truth (Psalm 145:18). The Lord is watching over you. You are always in the mind of Christ. I encourage you to be strong in the Lord. At times the burden will be heavy, but it will become lighter for you when you learn to cast your cares on the Lord.

I'm writing this book from the perspective of a woman, mom, and wife. This book is for the spouses, parents, children, family, and friends who serve as caregivers. To the husband who may take on the role as a caregiver, I speak strength unto you as you navigate this journey for your wife. There is no correct or wrong way to read this book. The purpose of this book is to bring encouragement, life, support, hope, and joy when your faith is being tested. I pray that you may learn from my experiences and know that you are not in this fight alone. God is right there; hold on to your faith. It is faith that keeps me together. Faith is right there in your corner.

I invite you to journey with me as I candidly share some of the woes, fears, anxiety, uncertainties, and mental, emotional, spiritual, and physical changes, as well as the progressions, accomplished tasks, joys, blessings, and miracles of being a spousal caregiver (which is what society calls it). I say I am called to be a helpmeet, which is what God calls it: *"And the Lord God said, 'It is not good that the man should be alone; I will make him an help meet for him'"* (Genesis 2:18). Eriq and I complement each other.

This book is a resource and reference to support you as a caregiver. Remember, this battle is not yours, it's the Lord's, for no one fights alone!

CHAPTER 1

ROUND 1 – THE FIRST DIAGNOSIS

> "This sickness is not unto death, but for the Glory of God that the son of God might be glorified thereby." (John 11:4; KJV)

JULY 2, 2007

The day started off as usual, fast-paced and full. I had taken the three youngest children to school. It was a Monday, so I headed to the office to do church administration duties, and Eriq went off to work. That evening, while at gymnastics class with our youngest daughter, Faith, who was nine, I received a phone call from my husband. He was not feeling well and was experiencing unbearable abdomen pain. He told me that his twin brother was going to take him to the emergency room and asked me to meet him there. I immediately began to call on the name of the Lord, for my God is omnipresent.

I knew at that point that something must not be right; he didn't ever want to go to the doctor. Now, a week before, my husband had finally shared with me that he'd seen blood in his stool. After he brought it to my attention a second time and said he was also in pain, I began to think, "Could this be a bleeding ulcer?" Immediately, I insisted he see the doctor and we scheduled a visit, but you know how it is with doctors' appointments. The visit was set for ten days later with the advice that, if his condition worsened, he should go to the emergency room. Well, two days before his scheduled appointment, the pain and blood returned.

As I headed to the hospital, traffic was everywhere. I began to take every shortcut I could think of while trying not to guess what the other possibilities were. In the meantime, Faith was wondering why we'd had to stop in the middle of her class, and she was hungry. So, I was looking for another route so that I could find a McDonald's. I met Eriq at the hospital; he said he was feeling better as I gave him a kiss on his forehead. He was given medication. An examination and a test revealed no presence of blood, and, with the pain subsiding, he was sent home and advised to take it easy. The emergency room doctor gave instructions for us to follow up with his primary. The appointment to see his primary doctor was set for eighteen days later. During that period, I would ask Eriq how he was feeling. He would reply, "I'm good." Although the pain and bleeding had ceased, I wondered whether he was really good. During the visit, the doctor examined Eriq and advised him to continue with the medication. He then proceeded to say, "Although you do not fall in the age range; I would like to schedule a colonoscopy with the gastroenterologist to complete a thorough exam." A colonoscopy is an exam that detects any abnormal findings in the large intestines and rectum.

JULY 25, 2007

The colonoscopy was performed to get an in-depth look and try to determine the cause of the pain in his abdomen and the bleeding. On the day of testing, something just did not feel right within me. I began to pray and sing to myself. I started off with the lyrics "You are my peace." As I sat in the waiting room, flipping through magazine after magazine, I began to wonder what was taking so long. I even asked the receptionist, "Is the procedure being done on another floor?"

Several hours later, a nurse came and told me the doctor wanted to see me for a moment. While waiting in a small office, I heard the Lord say, "This sickness is not unto death." I sat frozen in my chair. The nurse then called me a second time, saying the doctor was ready to see me.

The doctor came into the room and said to me, "The results do not look good; we have found some abnormalities."

I turned to him and asked, "What stage is it?"

The doctor looked at me strangely and asked, "Did my fellow doctor just talk to you?"

"No," I replied. For I knew that my doctor, the Holy Spirit, was just talking to me and preparing me. The abnormality in the test had been placed there to be found. A biopsy was performed shortly, and Eriq was returned to his room.

The doctor said to both of us, "As I was telling your wife, we saw a large mass and did a biopsy of your tissue. We will get back to the two of you as soon as we get the results."

At that point it seemed like I was okay. We embraced each other and left the consultation room. That was the longest walk ever to the parking lot, but I kept a smile on my face and maintained a conversation to keep Eriq's mind occupied. We sat in the car, prayed together, and drove home silently, creeping on the busy expressway. I was now at a loss for words. The doctors could not officially say that it was cancer because an analysis of the tissue had not been done.

On the ride home, I could hear the Holy Spirit speaking again: "My daughter, this sickness is not unto death, but for the Glory of God that the son of God might be glorified thereby" (John 11:4; KJV). So, as I replayed the Scripture that the Holy Spirit had just spoken and heard the doctor say, "We will do further testing," but never answer me when I asked what stage, my mind could only hear "cancer." I dared not say it out loud, though. That evening, we had dinner with the family, watched a movie together, prayed, and went to bed.

July 26, 2007 – Round 1

Can you imagine being woken up by a call from the doctor on the third day after testing to be given the news that you have stage 3 cancer? Well, that's what happened to my husband. I sat up in bed. My husband looked astonished on the phone, and then he fell to his knees from the side of the bed, saying, "No! No!" I was stunned when I heard the report. After the shock, I looked into my husband's eyes and said, "We will get through this. We are going to fight this and we are going to win." Then I thought to myself, *well why did the doctor have to tell us over the phone? What was he thinking?* Of course, I had a moment as the tears rolled down my face. *What do we do now? How do we deal with this?* It was now a fact that Eriq had been diagnosed with cancer, but the truth is stronger than facts, and the truth of the matter was that my God was a healer.

Albert Einstein said, "The world we have created is a product of our thinking: it cannot be changed without changing our thinking." And the Bible tells us, "For as a man thinketh in his heart so is he" (Proverbs 23:7; KJV). I quickly got up and said to my husband, "This battle is the Lord's." God said that, by His stripes, we were already healed (Isaiah 53:5). I believed the word of God. For part of that day, I went from sitting to lying in bed with our worship music on. I was in and out of prayer and said to myself, "God has no respect of a person, He will bring us out." I made sure that my phone line was open because I was waiting for the nurse to call me back with further instructions. Later that evening, I found myself drifting and in a pool of tears. I thought to myself, "I just want our life back like it was." The next few days involved consultation with the oncologist, radiologist, and surgeons to determine what would be the best approach. I was starting to feel overwhelmed with the back-to-back consultations and document after document, trying to line up insurance forms for the clearance of treatments.

I then did further research on stage 3 cancer, applying both natural and spiritual protocols. Naturally, I began to change how Eriq was eating. I sought out a nutritionist and drove forty-five minutes away from home in order to take classes on healthier meal plans; I learned how to substitute the foods that were not building the immune system with other foods that would bring him energy and strength so that his body would be able to handle the treatments from chemotherapy and radiation.

I began to make natural juices from fruits and vegetables. They were not easy for my husband to transition to, especially when he already had his favorite foods and drinks lined up. I felt that an urgent change, incorporating these items in his diet, would propel him closer to being healthy. By contrast, red meats and carbs would pile up and become toxic to his body; these were trigger factors during this time and would prolong the process. I could not imagine what was going through Eriq's mind. I prayed for peace and continued love for him while quoting the Scripture: *"For God has not given me the spirit of fear but of peace, love and a sound mind"* (2 Timothy 1:7). I then said to myself, "You have to be strong for Eriq and the family." My marriage vows had included the words "in sickness and in good health." I was so angry with the enemy that I told him (satan) that this weapon (cancer) would not prosper, after all, God's word said, *"No weapon formed against you shall prosper"* (Isaiah 54:17). I was also reminded of Ephesians 4:29, which said, *"Let no corrupt communication proceed out of your mouth, but that which is good to the use of edifying, that it may minister grace unto the hearers."*

I spoke life into my husband every day and night in spite of the doctors' reports, no matter what his test results revealed, and no matter how his physical appearance changed. When I received phone calls from family and friends, I found myself encouraging them.

I had to change my thinking. I was determined not to let any negative thought or behavior, or any negative influences from the outside come near my dwelling. I began to clean the house more to keep my mind occupied, for I was reminded of the Bible story about Jairus's daughter (Mark 5: 21–43). On the way to Jairus's home, Jesus stopped to heal a woman. When they arrived at the house, people told Jairus, "It's too late; she is dead." Jesus heard their words and immediately said, "Do not be afraid; just believe." Many people were crying over the death of the little girl. Jesus then said she was not dead but sleeping.

When our family and friends heard about my husband's condition, they, too, began to talk. No, he was not dying, but their negative talk and responses were death. I even had a parent from school stop me to say, "Oh, I saw your husband, and he doesn't look good. He has lost so much weight; you know, my grandmother died from cancer."

I immediately said, "It is not so; death shall not come near him. This sickness is not unto death, so if you cannot stand here and encourage me, then I would rather you keep silent." We parted ways. Her words had been frustrating to hear.

I even had some comment, "You are going through a lot. Your oldest daughter, Brittany, has gone away to New York for college, your youngest daughter has been accepted into a gifted school on the North Side, and then you have the boys. How are you going to do all that and the church?"

I simply replied, "I can't, but I can do all things through Christ Jesus who strengthens me, according to Philippians 4:13."

My sister would help out by taking the three younger children to school, while Eriq, Jr., was in high school. Specific duties were given to the ministerial team, and it kept the church afloat. It had only been five years since the ministry had started. We did not have a consistent person to handle the administration let alone the ability to hire one at their requested rate, so I took on the role. On Mondays, I did my administrative work for the church, so I would take my iPad to the treatment center.

Now let's return to the Bible story (Mark 5:21–43): As Jesus saw the people's fear, he had everyone except his disciples, Jairus, and his wife leave the home. Similarly, when negative talk came around Eriq, I immediately shut it out. I did not want his ear gates to hear anything or anyone that was not speaking life. My hope remained steadfast in the Lord.

My home was constantly saturated with worship music. I begin to screen all phone calls. I would not even allow people to bring over certain foods. It was not that I didn't appreciate the hospitality; I just didn't want him to consume any ingredients that would not nourish his cells and would disrupt the natural healing flow. I began to pray and to ask God what to do. We were able to incorporate some natural protocols with the medical treatments. As 1 Corinthians 15:46 stated, "Howbeit that was not first which is spiritual, but that which is natural; and afterward that which is spiritual" (KJV).

The natural body is flesh and blood, consisting of bones, muscles, nerves, veins, arteries, and fluids; hence, it is of a corruptible frame and form. It is liable to break down, decay, and deteriorate. I began to do research on the various types of food that cancer fed on. Every food that contributed to the vitality of cancer, I began to filter from my kitchen. Those foods were no longer on my grocery list. I even searched for and found an alternative nutrition center in Evanston, Illinois. We were able to include the foods that would strengthen his immune system.

As a familiar hymn says, "What can wash away my sin? Nothing but the blood of Jesus. What can make me whole again? Nothing but the blood of Jesus."

An adult of average size has a little less than 10 pints of blood according to *The World Book Rush-Presbyterian-St. Luke's Medical Center Medical Encyclopedia* (7th edition Chicago: World Book 1995). Blood is the fluid that transports nutrients and oxygen to the cells in your body. It also takes away waste from your body, fights infection, and carries chemicals that regulate many bodily functions.

In addition to natural change, I applied spiritual change. I applied the word. I spoke healing Scriptures and interceded for my husband. I prayed with and for my children. The children even prayed for their dad. I supported my husband and allowed him to participate as much as he could in activities with the children. I reminded God of His words that by His stripes we were healed (Isaiah 53:1). And I thought of 3 John 1:2, which said, *"Beloved, I wish above all things that thou mayest prosper and be in health, even as thy soul prospers."*

After we received the confirmed results of his stage 3 cancer diagnosis, everything began to move quickly. Three days after the notice, I left to go and speak at a women's conference. Our children had dentist's and doctor's appointments. Afterward, it would be necessary to go to the new elementary school for registration and to complete college freshman orientation forms. Eriq had to have various tests and lab work done to prepare for chemotherapy and radiation treatments. This lifestyle was becoming a part of our temporary new normal. Eriq was determined for it not to interrupt our daily lives. We drove our daughter twelve hours to New York, where she was about to start the next phase of her life as a college student. As she would be many miles away from home, we decided not to tell her the news until she came home for Thanksgiving.

On August 20, 2007, Eriq had outpatient surgery for the insertion of a port-a-cath. The port-a-cath is a proprietary indwelling device that provides long-term IV access for administering TPN, blood products, drugs, and high-dose chemotherapy. In a matter of seven days, daily chemotherapy and weekly radiation treatment began. I recall how awkward it was the very first day we walked into the treatment center. All eyes were on us. We were the youngest couple, the youngest people in the sitting area. The look we got said, "What are you two doing here!"

After twelve weeks of treatment, Eriq was exhausted, and I was exhausted; yet, whenever he turned to me, God would give me enough strength to smile back at him and say, "We can do it." Now, hear me; although he was the one going through the daily treatments, I felt every pain and groan. The radiation treatments also taxed his body.

Eriq's nutrition became unbalanced. He would have the desire and need to eat but be unable to eat. Moreover, his weight would drop uncontrollably. When we went to see the doctors, they would constantly say, "Eriq, you have to eat something." I understood what the doctors were saying. He had to eat something, so if he desired a burger, it would be ideal to let him eat that. At the same time, I thought the ingredients in the fast food would not help kill off the cancer cells. Yet the doctors would reassure me that the treatments would get rid of the bad cells. Well, cancer was not taking things lightly with him, and I wasn't taking things lightly with the food. So I was not going to allow any food in that would give the cancer cells ammunition. I would not feed him that red burger. I began to pray that his taste buds would line up and function with the perfection that God had intended.

There were times when the doctor would say, "You are at this stage and yet you are not experiencing the usual symptoms: sores in your mouth and even depression and uncontrollable anxiety. You are one of the very few patients I've seen that do not show the normal side effects from such a hard hit of chemo and radiation." The senior doctor thought that it was strange that the symptoms were not occurring and would say, "I know, I know; it's the man upstairs, right?"

My response would be "To God be the Glory!" To me, Eriq's condition was proof that naturally, the supplements and alkaline foods had helped lessen the adverse effects. It is worth mentioning a few of the side effects of the treatments that Eriq endured. He experienced the tingling, burning, and peeling of his hands and feet. Focusing on the natural, I would apply a mixture of Aquaphor® healing ointment with virgin olive oil, and focusing on the Spirit, I would apply the word of God. When Eriq experienced loss of appetite, I would make healthy smoothies that were infused with vitamins and minerals that would lessen the symptoms he was experiencing. I would cook his favorite foods using different herbs and pray as I stirred. I would speak to his internal organs before he ate and as he ate.

During his infusion treatments, the Lord would send people our way, even non-Christians, for us to minister to. According to Romans 15:1, *"We then that are strong, ought to bear the infirmities of the weak, and not to please ourselves."* So, even in my weakness as well as my husband's weakness, His strength was made perfect.

Throughout the treatments, surgeries, and physical changes to my husband's body, I never lost hope. I kept the faith. When his weight dropped dramatically, I would either buy new garments or take his favorite clothes for alteration. At times, when the enemy would try to come in and let me see my husband in his natural state, I would say, "Lord, I look unto the hills from whence comes my help; it all comes from you, Lord. Now, Lord, do what only You can do. Let me see my husband as You see him."

Early one morning, on **November 17, 2007,** I was awakened by the sound of Eriq moaning. I saw him sitting on the side of the bed as I began to call his name, but he would not answer. I could see him sitting there, gazing stone-faced into the air. I begin to shout his name: *"ERIQ!"* There was no response. He slowly began to slump over onto the bed. I dialed 911 as I called on Jesus. Frantically, I woke up the boys. I had an ache in my throat and my eyes began to fill up quickly as I clutched his body with one hand. I kept talking to my husband, reassuring him that it was going to be alright and asking him to stay with me. The paramedics arrived and I watched him as they took his vitals, saying that they had to move quickly. He was admitted into the emergency room. I sat there with sweaty, shaky hands, thinking that this could not be happening. At that moment, you couldn't tell my human mind that it was all good, "but [it was] working together for our good."

Prior to Thanksgiving, Eriq had surgery. Now, who could eat turkey at a time like that? I couldn't although I was thankful that the surgery went well. On December 21, 2007, I received the best early Christmas gift ever. Eriq was on the road to recovering well, and on January 8, 2008, another surgery was performed to close his ileostomy (according to the American Cancer Society, an ileostomy is an opening made in the abdomen during surgery). Those six months caused our stress levels to fluctuate on the Richter scale, but staying focused on the word of God kept us grounded. God showed up in that fight, and healing took place. The fight was worth it. My husband was cancer free. He was monitored regularly for the next three years as he returned back to work.

Why do people get sick? Why are some homeless? Why are there poor people? Why are some children orphans? Why do unfortunate things happen to good people? Why, why, why? "Why?" is a great question, and we could spend a great deal on what we think the answers could be. I even ask, "Why my husband, Lord? Why?" I can say for certain that, in this lifetime, we will experience some blows, heartache, injustice, death, inhumanity, sickness, pain, etc. None of that was part of God the Father's original plan (Romans 8:22). Our hope is in Jesus Christ, who lived, walked the earth, died, and rose again in order to redeem us. Be confident in knowing that, if you know Jesus Christ, then you know that He will never leave you or forsake you and that, when you are weak and weary, He will give unto you strength. Ask him today!

I thought I had to be strong not only for my husband and myself but also for our children and family. Boy, that was so not true. I only needed to wait on the Lord and to take heart in Him. God began to give me insurmountable strength that I knew was not my own. I continued to pray, fast, anoint my husband's body, and intercede for him. God gave me the grace to be there for my husband and family as well as for the church.

According to Isaiah 55:8, *"For my thoughts are not your thoughts, neither are my ways your ways,' saith the Lord."* Several weeks prior to the Apostle's sickness, the church was in transition, the leasing of property was taking a toll on the finances of the church, and, at the same time, we were asked to help to build and encourage another church. God had it all planned out; we were now in a place that allowed the congregation to be together in one place and in one accord while my husband was going through treatments. While the church helped minister to another church in their time of need, God met our needs. I did not have time to worry because the Bible said, *"Take therefore no thought for the morrow: for the morrow shall take thought for the things of itself. Sufficient unto the day is the evil thereof"* (Matthew 6:34).

God is so awesome; in the midst of everything that was going on, He kept my mind. Isaiah 26: 3 (KJV), says it best: *"Thou will keep him in perfect peace whose mind is stayed on thee: because he trusteth in thee."* I thank God for my sister and mother, who helped out tremendously with the kids, as well as my mother-in-law. I was blessed to have church members and families who would come and get the kids and take them out so that they could keep engaging in their daily activities.

I give all the glory and honor to God for manifesting His healing power. I say to you, stand still and see the salvation of the Lord. I reminded the Lord that, according to Isaiah 55:11, He said, *"So shall my word be that goeth forth out of my mouth: it shall not return unto me void, but it shall accomplish that which I please, and it shall prosper in the thing whereto I sent it."* The Lord sent His word and healed him. Hallelujah!

CHAPTER 2

ROUND 2 – THE SECOND DIAGNOSIS

> "But as for you, ye thought evil against me; *but* God
> meant it unto good, to bring to pass, as *it is* this day,
> to save much people alive." (Genesis 50:20)

Eriq and I were both in the best of health over the next ten years. The year 2017 was distinctive and was most certainly going to be memorable. Eriq and I were embarking on twenty-five years of marriage. Our last child was in his final year of high school. Life was going well for the family and me. A few days to the end of February, my husband started experiencing chest pain. We weren't too concerned; he thought he might have strained a muscle from playing sports earlier that week or might have a common cold with mild congestion due to the fall season. The cough lingered for a few days; a call was made to our primary. Next came blood work, an X-ray, and instructions to rest with fluids and wait to pick up a bronchodilator from the doctor. Eriq was living his everyday life with work outside the home, and church activities continued.

In **March 2017,** a week later, it was time for Eriq's follow-up. The doctor wanted to see how the bronchodilator had been managing the mild congestion. Eriq was on his way to work, so he insisted that I didn't need to go. He would swing by the doctor's on the way to work. It turned out the X-ray results were displaying haziness to the left side of his chest. Immediately, a CT scan was ordered. Less than two hours later, a call from Eriq woke me up. He said, "Hold on. I'm putting the doctor on the phone to talk to you." I felt terrible for not being there with him.

The CT scan revealed that the shadow on his lower lung was a mass sitting next to his aorta, and the blood vessels were enlarged. A bronchoscopy (a procedure done using a thin tube with a tiny camera attached to one end; the tube is inserted into the lungs to explore them and the air passages) was performed. Eriq's cancer had resurfaced, and it was trying to establish residency in his lung. We sat and prayed, processing another battle. Even with the second diagnosis, we did not doubt the Lord would do the impossible: *"God is not a man, that he should lie"* (Numbers 23:19). One doctor even mentioned that it might be best to remove the entire left lobe. Continuous prayers and fasting were done, followed by in-depth consultation with medical professionals. A second opinion was sought because the initial surgeon wanted to skip all treatments and remove the lung. The doctors agreed that Eriq's body was healthy despite the spot on his lung, so we decided to go with the treatments to shrink the tumor first because it was pushing up against his arteries.

Eriq would undergo chemotherapy and radiation treatment and surgery, which would yield a good report: remission from lung cancer.

Well, would you like to know how I handled this one? I sat, frozen in place in the doctor's office, as the adrenaline rushed through my body. I tried to compose myself; inside, I screamed, "JESUS! Not again! He never even smoked!" This round was a lung metastasis diagnosis. "Lord, we need you," I prayed. So, once again, we stepped into the ring and approached cancer using fighting words: that the blood of Jesus would prevail.

Knowing that God was in control this second time, cancer tried to send my life out of control. This one here really tried to permeate my mind. I asked myself, "Where did I go wrong? How did I miss the warning signs? What were they?" But I could only answer myself and say, "Oh Lord; you are the same today, yesterday, and forevermore." The terrible disease is trying to establish another way in.

Ten years after the first diagnosis, we were back to a familiar routine. We would enter the treatment center. Blood work would be drawn first to see if Eriq's body could endure the medication. Sometimes this would take longer than usual if the phlebotomist forgot to check the labs within the appropriate time frame. While we waited for thirty minutes to receive the results, the oncologist would check to see how everything was going and how Eriq had been feeling. The nurse would then review a list of questions about his appetite, assess his mental and emotional levels, determine what new issues had occurred, and make sure all the documents were up to date and cleared.

During this round of cancer, the oncology doctors had to switch chemotherapy medication. It was a different round from the first. Eriq could not touch anything cold, and the side effects of the neuropathy he was experiencing intensified, so the first half of the treatments were challenging. Yet he kept a smile on his face and prayed for the other cancer patients. Despite the new side effects he experienced, he was able to avoid slightly more of the severe side effects, which sounded grueling and painful when the oncologist asked him about them.

I remember coming home one evening. A spirit of heaviness walked in with me. I immediately called on Jehovah Shalom, declaring that I had the mind of Christ. I then called a few of my close friends, asking them to come by. These powerful women of God came, surrounded me, sat, listened, and comforted me as I began to pour out. My eyes were red, and my knees toppled to the floor and bent as the dam suddenly broke. I cried; I wailed, letting go and letting God: *"But the Lord is faithful, who shall establish you and keep **you** from evil"* (2 Thessalonians 3:3). I had to let my "Yes, Lord," be "Yes, Lord."

Because my thought process was out of alignment, my distorted fears had become latent and were in the process of depleting me: "This can't be happening; I'm his helpmate, so how did I let the re-fearing, re-evidence, re-appearance, and re- realization of false belief surface?" At one point, I found myself switching from one assignment to another. My repetitive activities were merely a cover-up of my attempts to escape. From the outside looking

19

in, no one would ever have known what I was going through if I had not told you.

A loud voice in my mind said. "This cancer is not like the first; how will you handle this one?" I lost sleep at night, propped up in bed, listening to my husband's wheezing. The enemy was trying to gain ground in my mind, and I was determined not to let that manifest. Every time a crackling, hissing sound emerged from Eriq's chest, I would say, "The blood of Jesus." I would declare the word of the Lord that I had a sound mind. God tells us numerous times not to fear because He is the one in control. He is our refuge and strength. Worry and fear are not of the Lord. Did I forget who my God was? No, but when you let an issue overpower you, even for a moment, you give false accusations the opportunity to occur. So, it was up to me to bring the complaint against the enemy before the courts of Heaven, allowing Jesus to testify on my behalf. The Bible tells us that the spirit of prophecy is the testimony of Jesus (Revelation 19:10). Let the word speak!

I had to be still and listen . Amid the chatter, I could not hear the quiet voice say, "Rest, trust, and only believe." The enemy's voice is always louder than the voice of God because the enemy is trying to get your attention. It's natural to turn to a loud sound quicker than you would turn to a soft voice. That's the enemy's trick: sending out subliminal messages that will try to steal, kill, and destroy. The Teacher is always silent during the test and says in a gentle voice, "But I come that you may have life and have it more abundantly." I'm so glad that I did not let that loud, clanking voice overshadow me.

So how did I change that reaction? I had to position myself and say, "Hold fast to your faith without wavering." I prayed for my thoughts to only focus on an excellent report; I went to bed with praise and woke up with a song of thanksgiving. In my prayer, I had to consciously affirm with the mind of Christ that every plant of cancer, fatigue, and fear that the Father did not plant would be uprooted in Jesus's name and that by His stripes we were healed.

The Bible character, David, tells us to put our trust in God when we are afraid. So, if you are faced with life circumstances, praise Him when your heart is heavy. My husband would tell me, "We are going to make it through this one as well." Although he was the one with the illness, I was indirectly affected. God gave him strength at that moment to turn around and become my caregiver and encourage me on the journey. So, when I was at 40%, feeling inadequate for the assignment, God gave my husband the other 60% to pull us through. Similarly, when my husband was at 10% or even less with the side effects of the immunotherapy, Jesus would equip me with the 90% to carry us through. Praise was our weapon.

During the latter half of the treatment, the children were back in school with extracurricular activities. As long as he was feeling up to it, Eriq would be right there in the stands with extra layers of clothing on so he would not feel the adverse impact of the air conditioner. Seeing the boy's playing basketball was priceless to him. Some would say that I should have insisted that my husband not go to the games. Was I wrong for letting him go? I wanted Eriq to do what he enjoyed doing as long as he had the strength and stamina to do it, and when he needed to rest, he rested.

I admired my husband because, as long as he had energy in his body, he would go to church and stand in the pulpit to share an encouraging word with the people. There were times when I wanted him to stay in, but I knew that he would say, "As long as I can stand, this 'cold' is going to have to stand with me or leave my body now." Cold was a word my husband would use in place of cancer. If you could see him when he made it to the podium, you would have seen how Jesus gave him another breath of fresh air to go on. After church was over, we would go home, allowing him to rest and replenish his energy. God had already declared our end from the beginning. We grew so close that, when one of us was hurt, the other would feel their pain.

The Cross Punch and Jab

So during round two of the fight, a cross punch was directed at me. One night, I awoke to a burning sensation in my feet. It was traveling up my legs. I sat on the side of the bed, hearing my heart thud in my chest; it felt like it was closing up on the left side. I remained calm as the sensation was magnified. I tried to stand up and reach for aspirin or ibuprofen as the water dripped from my face: "It's not there!" I staggered to the edge of the bed. My husband woke up, saw me in distress, and called 911. The quiet house was now in a state of disarray. My balance was like that of a seesaw. Every time I put my foot on the floor, a fiery bolt of lightning would travel from my toes to my calf. I tried to explain what was going on in my body, but the words were not intelligible; I could only get up, feet burning. I had never felt this way before. I didn't know how to stop it! I demonstrated another level of trust in God: I repeatedly thought, "This will be okay."

The paramedics arrived and prepared to transport me to the nearest hospital. Eriq was standing outside the ambulance. As I looked over, I saw his face was flushed and he was beginning to lose his balance. I shouted to the paramedics, "Please help!" Eriq's pressure had dropped, and he appeared dizzy. The paramedics attended to us both while sending in the dispatch. As the paramedics' door closed, the thought of leaving Elijah, Faith, and Emanuel standing outside the ambulance was unbearable.

We were taken to a community hospital nearby. Our children had made their way to the hospital. Eriq's pressure had returned to baseline, and I sat with an oxygen mask on and my feet still burning. I was concerned about him, and he was worried about me. God was concerned about us both. While receiving IV fluids and pain medications, I lay in the hospital bed thinking, "Now, what is this all about?" Hours later, the test results came back. They were inconclusive.

God knows everything about us. God already knew that, on that night, both of us would end up in the ambulance. We could not be shaken by what was occurring. Though I didn't understand, I knew that, somehow, it was all working for our good. Jesus will meet you right where you are and administer what you need. We were able to overcome that distraction. So, my friend, when sickness and doubt plague your mind, do not succumb to them. Stop nursing those head injuries and the diagnosis of worry, wounds, fear, anxiety, and panic attack: *"Peace I leave with you, my peace I give unto you: not as the world giveth, give I unto you. Let not your heart be troubled, neither let it be afraid"* (John 14:27).

Negative situations will occur, distracting you. Repeat the process of declaring, *"For God hath not given us the spirit of fear; but of power, and of love, and of a sound mind"* (2 Timothy 1:7). Eriq continued with the protocols. Not only were we praying for other patients that were receiving treatment, but the oncologist himself was also asking for prayer. The assignment to pray for the doctor and other patients that we came in contact with kept our attention on Jesus Christ and His love. We were no longer dwelling on our circumstances, for things changed when we prayed!

We kept praising God for His goodness and giving Him thanks for who He was and what He had already done. Within God's timing, we witnessed the manifestation of God's healing power in Eriq's life. We continued with the doctor visits while decreeing daily, speaking over his life, saying only what the word of God said: "Heaven and earth shall pass away, but the word of God shall stand firm forever" (Matthew 24:35). I played these words over in my mind, that the Lord sent to heal us. We had obtained the strength to cope with another round of treatments. By his wounds we were healed (Isaiah 53:5). Hallelujah!

September 2017 was the last day of the treatments. After two months of rest, Eriq was eager to return to work for a few weeks right before the winter break.

It was now **January 2018**. Almost a year before, we had received the second diagnosis. This was the last follow-up with the radiation doctor. There was no infection or inflammation in the lungs. Eriq's body was free of cancer.

I want to share a note of double victory: During this illness, our church was in the process of purchasing the location that we had been leasing for several years. On the day of signing for the church, my husband was scheduled to remove his chest port. We woke up early and went to the hospital; my brother-in-law was right there with us. I stayed until I saw Eriq back in recovery with his eyes open, kissed him on the forehead, and said, "You are incredible!" That was the name our youngest daughter had given her dad: Mr. Incredible. Eriq's brother stayed behind to monitor him, while one of the board members and I went to the property purchase closing. That day, we received two keys, one key for our church home and the other key for the healing of my husband, our Apostle.

CHAPTER 3

ROUND 3 – OVERWHELMED TO OVERJOYED

> "Cast thy burden upon the LORD, and he shall sustain thee: he shall never suffer the righteous to be moved." (Psalm 55:22)

JANUARY 2020

The year 2020 was a year that no one globally would ever forget. Covid-19 had made its way to the United States, and the atmosphere was full of uncertainty. It was heading towards pandemic status. In the later part of January, at the break of dawn, my husband woke me up and said, "Lay your hands right here. There's a sharp pain that has been lingering throughout the night." I immediately began to pray that every negative assignment that was causing the pain would be relinquished by his body in Jesus's name. As my husband arose from the bed, he headed to the restroom. I became uneasy because the fact that my husband was describing this pain to me indicated that it had been occurring on and off for some time. Quickly turning to the side of the bed, I begin to pray and thank God for His wonderful working power. I asked God to give me a revelation. In the midst of uncertainty, our faith remained strong. We had been carried through two rounds of cancer. I thought, "My God, my husband does not look like what he has been through! God is a keeper of the mind and body!" Now Eriq was left with some battle scars; I just looked at them as a reminder of what my God could do. The Lord is no respecter of persons; we have all been given a set time.

FEBRUARY 6, 2020

The doctor visit led to the scheduling of a PET scan. A few days later, a scan report revealed to us abnormal findings; there was a spot was on top of Eriq's right adrenal gland, the dreadful disease called cancer was on the prowl. As you may have noticed, I said, "We received the report." The Bible says, *"So they are no longer two, but one flesh. Therefore what God has joined together, let no one separate"* (Matthew 19:6). We did everything together; we prayed together, we laughed together and cried together. You get it, right? We even went through Eriq's sickness together. I attended all his doctor's appointments and participated in the process of treatment and the healing and recovery just as I had with the previous ones.

You may be wondering how I handled the third round. I prayed, "Jesus, You carried us through the previous ones; I know You will carry us through this one." We came together and agreed upon the word of the Lord, declaring God's promises for healing. I said to my husband, "Yet in all these things we are more than conquerors through Him who loved us" (Romans 8:37). Throughout the fight called cancer, our lives were a living testimony. Staying focused was important.

So I took the report to God in prayer, and HE gave me peace that surpassed all understanding. "Shalom" is a word that stands for peace in the Bible. During round three, for a human moment, I was numb yet more at ease and with a more peaceful and renewed outlook than I'd had with the other two diagnoses.

I did feel a little lump beginning to lodge itself in my throat. I inhaled and said, "Shalom." The New Testament tells us that the *shalom* of God deals with all things being reconciled to God and that he is pleased. Shalom is not limited to just one aspect of your life. Shalom covers you spiritually, mentally, physically, socially, and economically. Shalom talks about having a right relationship with the Father and with others. Shalom, the peace of God, can only come from God. The peace of God stands above all doubt, fear, anxiety, worry, and uncertainty and the difficult moments that we face in life. In this round, no chemotherapy or radiation was given. I was elated! God knew everything and was already aware of the outcome.

MARCH 6, 2020

On the day of Eriq's surgery, the sun was shining, and he was feeling fine and ready for the surgery to start and ultimately end. I was calm and confident that it was a good day as we prepared to go to the hospital. Then my body started flaring up again. The symptoms of the tingling and burning sensations in my limbs had returned. I began to pray and to say, "I don't have time for you, so leave my presence in Jesus's name." I applied oil to my body and took a Tylenol while we were on our way. My brother-in-law accompanied us to the hospital, and we checked into the preoperative unit. We all prayed, laughed, and chatted while waiting for the anesthesiologist. After Eriq was fully prepped and the IV was inserted, I gave him a kiss on the forehead, and his brother and I were directed to the waiting room.

I sat with my brother-in-law, talking, watching TV, and drinking cold coffee in the cold room to stay awake. Several hours had gone by; the receptionist should have been calling us to go see Eriq in Recovery. But his patient number did not flash across the monitor. I was not moved; I began to pray. Another hour went by, and we were told to head to the recovery room. I was looking forward to seeing Eriq. He was drowsy, and I was glad to see him and to get a good report: The surgery had been a success. He was placed in a room for overnight observation. The nurse allowed me to stay in the guest area for the night, right outside their station, which was next to Eriq's room. As I sat in my chair, reading, and thanking God for the victory, pins and needles traveled up my legs. There was numbness in my upper limb. What was going on! I began to quote Isaiah 53:5. Somewhat relieved because I was sitting outside the nurse's station, I tried to keep my mind off what was happening to me. I went back and forth, checking on my husband throughout the night. I did not want to concern him with the symptoms I was experiencing as I felt we didn't need another disruptor. The symptoms finally subsided as I lay on the sofa listening to music. The next morning, Eriq was given a clean bill of health and sent home to continue his recovery until the follow-up. A week later, we met again with the surgeon and were told that all was well and only an annual visit would be needed. Eriq was not my other half but my better half.

I am ever grateful to God for manifesting His healing power. I am also grateful that the procedure was done right before Covid-19 was declared a pandemic. We were able to go in and receive treatment as usual. No masks were required, and the visits we were accustomed to were allowed. Through it all, God continued to manifest His power in our lives. Throughout Eriq's sickness, we were blessed not to have to endure hardship or lack for anything. Our family remained united; the church family was even closer and very supportive.

Throughout all three rounds of the fighter's fight of faith, my husband was able to regain strength and do all that he was called to do and much more! We experienced the wholeness of God: nothing missing, nothing lacking. During that journey, I went from feeling mentally overwhelmed to overjoyed. We learned to live in the now. On the days when my husband was at his best, we had outings and enjoyed each other to the fullest. We learned to cherish the moments while allowing the morrow to come—one day at a time.

But something was wrong.

MARCH 2020

Over the next several months, I started to have symptoms that ranged from mimicking polycystic ovarian syndrome to mimicking type 2 diabetes. A battery of tests was administered, and there were visits to other specialists, who tried to resolve the issue.

One evening, while I was at home watching a movie, my chest began to tighten as if someone was squeezing me. My heart was racing as if I was getting into the starting blocks, and it felt as if the gun went off. My heart rate began to intensify. A weird feeling came over my left arm. The tingling in my arms felt like something crawling under and pricking at my skin. I sat still, speechless and afraid to move; tears rolled down my face as I experienced pain. My husband turned from watching the movie as I sat with a clenched fist to my chest. Immediately, he started to pray. He decreed that the pain would dissipate as I sat, taking deep breaths. My husband said that, if it didn't get better by a certain time, I would be going to the hospital. As the days progressed, I felt like I was on a tidal wave with intermittent palpitations and nausea. I experienced insomnia because a roaring sound developed in my ear and would not let up. My husband would lay hands on me and pray as I drifted off to sleep. The tests all came back inconclusive, and, with every pain, I would hear, *"For I will restore health unto thee, and I will heal thee of thy wounds,' says the Lord"* (Jeremiah 30:17).

The insulin in my body had become resistant. According to WebMD (2005–2021), insulin resistance occurs when the cells in your muscles, fat, and liver do not respond well to insulin and, therefore, cannot use glucose from your blood for energy. Some risk factors of insulin resistance are high blood pressure, low exercise, smoking, sleep issues, and obesity. The doctor thought that maybe my persistent sleep issues and decreased daily routine were contributing to insulin resistance. If it was left untreated, complications could occur that would cause harm and compromise my health. The Bible tells us that He empowers the feeble and infuses the powerless with strength (Isaiah 40:29). Know that God is not disappointed in your weakness. Your weakness is like a stage where the Glory of God shines His spotlight, manifesting miracles, signs, and wonders.

Heeding this warning regarding my health, I began to exercise daily and to change my eating habits. Being consistent with an alkaline diet, sleep, and an increase in exercise were key factors that dictated my well-being. I asked the Lord to show me the foods that would replenish and revive my body. The food preparation classes that I had taken years before when Eriq had first been diagnosed prepared me to make the change more apparent in my life. I was now on the road to my healing; I felt much better and had to learn to listen when my body said to rest. After all, even Jesus left the crowd behind to retreat.

You should be okay with getting that alone time, for it will bring about a renewed mind. Was it wrong for Jesus to get away? In the book of Mark 4, Jesus knew that there was an assignment to be completed. He knew that there were multitudes of people that needed healing, deliverance, and breakthrough. Did Jesus forget to attend to the needs of these people? Jesus was not insensitive to the people, yet, at that very moment, He needed to rest. Jesus Himself grew tired from a long day and found rest in the stern of a boat. You should learn this lesson from Jesus. When you feel tense and tired, find yourself a quiet place and rest. While at rest, you can lean on God for strength and guidance for the days to come. The problem in my life was that I was not getting enough sleep. The World Health Organization has termed "burnout" a medical condition. Not having a work–life balance can affect those ranging from workers in corporate America to stay-at-home moms. Our work with rest routines can yield more of a productivity balance and be effective as caregivers.

PRAYER

Heavenly Father, help me to remain constant in seeking You first in everything I do. Please help me not to feel rushed in my time with You. I will not focus on the problem; allow me to stay faithful to Your promises and blot out the chatter. For, at times, when I do not hold fast to Your security, I begin to worry. You are more significant than any ailment, and You are more extensive than any tasks or circumstances that may come my way.

Infuse me with Your Strength. There is no situation that YOU cannot handle. Just as David did, I cry out unto Thee because my heart is overwhelmed, leading me to the rock which is so much bigger than I. You oh, Lord, You are my strong tower. Thank You, Lord, for opening my spiritual ear gates so that I may hear You when you tell me to dial back, and that it is okay. Please help me put the various choices through Your filter prioritized the time needed for each task. For You, oh Lord, You are my strength!

Called to Care

CHAPTER 4

THE CHARGE OF A CAREGIVER

One way or another, we all have served, continue to serve, and/or will serve in many roles as caregivers. A former first lady of the United States and founder of The Carter Center, Rosalyn Carter, believes that there are four types of people: "those who have been caregivers, who are caregivers, who will be caregivers, and who will need caregivers" (Rosalynn Carter Institute for Caregivers, 2020).

There are many types of family caregivers: spousal, professional, volunteer, informal, friend or neighbor, and virtual caregivers. Who are these caregivers? Well, we all are. There is no age barrier: A family member, friend, or professional gives care to support the patient's health, well-being, and quality of life. Caregivers give support to those who have physical, psychological, or developmental needs. When my oldest daughter was fifteen months old, her language development started to regress, resulting in a medically confirmed diagnosis of hearing-impairment. This introduced a new caregiving role into my life. The learning of sign language and auditory speech began, for her and the family, sign language was introduced. I was both mother and advocate.

The caregiver extends themselves beyond their pain point and positions themselves to aid others. Caregivers take on tasks ranging from the smallest jobs to the biggest assignments in the short term and long term. When friends of mine had surgery, I was an informal caregiver, assisting in delivering their meals and picking up their medical supplies and medication from the pharmacy. Moreover, I assisted family members with their daily routine care and provided transportation to clinic visits. In addition, I professionally provided care to patients in the hospital. Individuals may help out or several family and friends may all pitch in together.

THE LIFE OF A CAREGIVER

Humility is the heart of a caregiver. There is no price tag on the uncalculated time, love, and support that they give. My love for helping and being supportive to my husband, family, and friends has always kept me on the front lines, looking for explanations of what they were going through. Family caregivers wear many hats. You may never have thought of yourself as a caregiver, but if you have ever gone to the grocery store for someone who was unable to, picked up someone's prescription, driven them to the clinic, done their after-school pick-up, dropped off a meal for them, communicated with medical staff, prepared their meals, handled their finances, assisted in their daily activities, or housed an aging parent, you are a caregiver. As the caregiver, you may be a part of the care recipient's day-to-day life, you may provide care by way of a phone call, or you may even live in another state.

Caregivers are qualified to become conscious of those they may serve. Whether the roles are personal or professional, paid or voluntary, caregivers have a special place in their hearts that has been designed to propel and preserve them.

THE QUALITIES OF A CAREGIVER

To name a few, one should possess patience, focus, and compassion and be personable and dependable. When you care for someone, you show kindness and concern towards them. Compassion entails sharing in the feelings of another to the point where you can understand and acknowledge how they are feeling. You recognize the suffering of the other and then take action to help with their situation.

Compassion requires inner discipline. I recall passing by a stranger that wanted money to buy food. At that particular time, I had just come from the store. I pulled over and gave them some of my groceries. In the Bible, Joseph was sold into slavery by his brothers; later on, they needed food, and Joseph provided it without any thought of what they had done to him. Furthermore, when Jesus saw that Lazarus's friends were mourning for his death, he was deeply moved by their grief and raised Lazarus from the dead. Mercy is a gift that one gives to another who is suffering when one responds to them with compassion.

As a caregiver, you can model the compassionate and merciful characteristics of Christ and others, sharing your love, compassion, and time. To become sensitive to the needs of the care recipient, the caregiver must listen to what the care recipient is saying or not saying. This is key—having an ear to hear that which is spoken naturally and that which is from the Lord.

The Bible says that there is no greater love than laying down your life for another (John 15:13). Two of the greatest commandments are to love God and to love your neighbor. We are not commanded to love ourselves, but it is understood that it is natural for one to love oneself. Caregiving is all about developing a relationship with yourself, God, and others.

THE CALL OF A CAREGIVER

Caregivers have strength and endurance in different areas. The caregiver willingly renders help to others in need. God will call you during various seasons in your life to care for others. Each time we are called to care, we are stretched and pushed further into new areas, engaging the abilities and talents that were lying dormant within us. Whenever I was called to care for others, I would end up appreciating the little things in life that I'd taken for granted. It does not matter what place you are at, know that you have been called to care!

The caregiver has just entered a new door to assist, guide, and take one through the disarray of a temporary, permanent, sudden, or slow onset of injury, illness, disability, or old age. Given the various possible circumstances and situations, there are different types of responses to give. A caregiver's day is never the same as the previous one. You will experience highs and lows, cries and laughter, and predictable and unpredictable days ahead.

THE CAREGIVER'S PRAYER

Father, help me to be the caregiver that You have called me to be. I acknowledge that, within myself, I cannot do this alone, but it is in You that I live, move, and have my being. Shine on me and through me. Show me what to do and then how You want me to do it. Saturate me with Your love till it overflows in me that I may be able to pour it out to others. Continue to let compassion abound in moments when I may feel overwhelmed. When I am weak, I ask You to strengthen me so that I may be a blessing to them. I pray that there will be no setbacks and that You will help me to walk in grace and see the sacred in every moment. Bless me to be patient and understanding with this process, for the manifestation of healing is in Your hands and in Your timing. God, send your agape love.

Thank You for trusting me with the role of a caregiver.

Life's Ups & Downs

CHAPTER 5

THE HEART OF A CAREGIVER

> "Let not your heart be troubled, neither
> let it be afraid." (John 14:27 b)

I think we sometimes underestimate the challenges that come with caregiving. As a result, we are not prepared for the difficulties we face, and we sometimes lose patience. I am not saying that, if we prepare, we will never be frustrated or impatient. But, when we acknowledge that caregiving brings both joys and frustrations, we can prepare ourselves for the difficult times.

— "Ask Dr. Amy," CaregiverStress.com

Many caregivers meet anxiety, stress, fear, and guilt. After an unexpected diagnosis, confusion, disbelief, and frustration may come. They can persist to the point where they interfere with daily activities; the caregiver may feel like they have very little to no control of what's going on around them. A spouse caregiver can even begin to cry out in deep distress due to their loved one's illness. Just as anxiety is a response to fear, worry is a natural response to stress. We have all experienced mild anxiety, for instance, when preparing for a test or a presentation to our boss. There are various degrees of anxiety, and some need treatment to become manageable. According to the National Institute of Mental Health (NIMH), women experience anxiety more than men. Anxiety tends to have similar symptoms to stress, for instance, insomnia, irritability, fatigue, and difficulty focusing. It can attack us by targeting our hearts and minds. Anxiety will try to sit on your sofa, dictating how bad it is and how you should feel about it. Anxiety exists on a continuum that ranges from everyday worries to chronic anxiety, which can cripple you in the long run. It's not just the person with the diagnosis who is in sorrow but also those around them.

The Bible tells us not to be anxious and that we should pray to make our request (Isaiah 41:10) when a problem arises. Admit to what you are feeling because prayer is your secret arsenal against anxiety: *"What time I am afraid, I will trust in thee"* (Psalm 56:3).

Being consistent in your prayer walk and regularly laying your anxiety at the foot of Jesus can erase the tension. Store up scriptures in your mind daily. Thus, when the crisis arises and the negative story wants to take center stage in your mind, God's word is right there to perform: *"Thou hast well seen, for I will hasten My word to perform it"* (Jeremiah 1:12). Recite the words from God's script, drawing on every truth to bring about healing and peace in your mind: *"Fear thou not; for I am with thee"* (Isaiah 41:10); I am victorious (1 Corinthians 15:57).

Remember, anxiety comes from a place of lack, which tries to get you to believe that you are not worthy and that there isn't enough for what you need. Anxiety occurs when you look at the situation without including God in it along with his promises. I didn't realize it initially, but during my husband's first encounter with cancer, I once encountered a spirit of fear and anxiety due to lack of control. I would not make plans as I could hear a voice say that I would become a widow. I remember that, when we went to purchase a car, I was unable to express excitement because all I wanted was for my husband not to have to go through the disease. I did not want to schedule any plans because I did not want the interruptions, so I had to relinquish control daily. I was grateful to God that the sentiment went away quickly. I reminded myself that I had every right to take that thought captive.

Foster an attitude of gratitude. Gratitude will interrupt the lack that lies in your mind. Say out loud, "Jehovah Jireh, You are my provider, You are more than enough for me. Say to yourself, "I can do all things through Christ Jesus who strengthens me." Say to yourself, "I am right. You are not in control. God is." Immerse yourself in the love of God.

Stress occurs when an outside source fuels your emotions; it's how both your brain and body respond to any demand. The body's natural response is to kick into the "fight or flight" mode. This helps the body to respond to the situation. Stress can be positive, keeping you focused and alert so that you can avoid the dangers ahead. It becomes problematic when it continues without relief or moments of regrouping and relaxation. Stress can be affected by something new and shocking that has occurred in your life; it can even occur when something physical has happened to you or someone dear to you.

Stress is alleviated when the situation is dealt with and resolved. The person under stress experiences both mental and physical symptoms. Some physical symptoms include aches and pains, a weak immune system, chest pain or a racing heart, exhaustion, headaches, tension in the muscles, digestive problems, an upset stomach, high blood pressure, and headaches. Stress can be short- or long-term, positive or negative. Outside caregiving, you may have a deadline or goal to meet. It may cause you to burn the midnight oil or result in changes in your sleep pattern, affecting your ability to focus. Everyone handles situations differently.

Anxiety and stress can overlap because they are emotional responses and can affect daily activities involving your mind and body. Diagnosis with an illness can lead to both the caregiver and care recipient becoming despondent. The healthy one becomes an ill caregiver. The things you were accustomed to doing and places you would normally have gone to have changed. Little things like walking in the sun were normal, but after treatment, the sun could have become taxing. Learning to accept the new normal and finding ways to make it comfortable can be a challenge. As a caregiver, you must embrace your new way of living.

I was trying to handle the situation on my own, and, therefore, I was losing. Was I frustrated at not being able to control the sickness? Did I feel guilty at times that I could not relieve my husband's pain? Did I somehow feel the situation was my fault? Now, I know I did not cause the cancer, but, when your loved one has been attacked, you feel you should have intervened in some way. When you have a ringside seat to a fight, it can lead to grief because, whenever you witness traumatic blows to your person, you feel those blows. With every alarming adverse reaction that my husband experienced, I found myself on edge. As I was trying to maintain my composure in front of him, I had to speak those things that were not as though they were. Although I am a pastor's wife and believe in God's healing, I was also human. The Lord tells us to let Him fight our battle and that we are not to lean on our understanding but trust Him.

I know you have the best interest of the person you are caring for at heart, and you feel the weight of being the responsible one. You do not want to fail. I had to realize that things were not going to go back to the way they had been. I had to embrace the new. The Bible tells me that, each day, God gives us brand new mercies (Lamentations 3:22–23). So, I began to wake up and look for the new normal every day. This is the air I breathe.

I want to share with you that it is ok if you cannot fix or do everything; in fact, the Holy Spirit wants you to be in that position so that you can rely on Him. God never said that we should depend on ourselves to carry the weight. You cannot look at your situation and then at your ability. The only answer that can bring these thoughts to a complete halt is resting in the arms of Jesus, knowing that He is right there and that He has freed us from all fears. Look to Jesus for joy. God did not promise that He would remove trials and tribulations. The Lord will do one of two things: He will either shield us from the current suffering or strengthen us in the suffering. At times we may be perplexed, but no matter what it looks like, we are not defeated (Proverbs 24:16).

Did you know that there were those in the Bible who also experienced the weight? Look at Moses: He was assigned to lead the Israelites from Egypt. Even when the Israelites disobeyed him and failed to understand the many struggles they faced, he accomplished the assignment that God had sent him to fulfill. Joseph was talked about, humiliated, and punished by being sent to jail to remember the trouble he experienced. Ester was convinced that the way out for her people was for her to go before the king, knowing that it might even cost her own life. I believe Paul experienced the most stress of them all. He was persecuted, suffered many shipwrecks, was abandoned by all his friends, was imprisoned, was bitten by snakes, and often went without food and shelter. That was quite a bit of suffering.

So how did Paul handle all of that? Well, he constantly reminded himself of the word of God: "My grace is sufficient" (2 Corinthians 12:9). This was where Paul was able to obtain his strength in times of weakness. We, too, can have Paul's mindset while going through life's challenges so that we may be strengthened. We need to be renewed over and over (as many times as it may take) by the constant ringing of God's word in our ears, telling us that Jesus Christ, His sovereign grace, will give unto us all the stability, nourishment, and peace of mind that we need. At times we look for solutions to our situations on our own, and nothing seems to work out. Life's lesson to us is that we should turn it over to Jesus; find our strength in Him alone. John 16:33 puts it best: *"I have told you these things, so that in me you may have peace. In this world, you will have trouble. But take heart! I have overcome the world."*

CHAPTER 6

THE MIND OF A CAREGIVER

> "Not that I speak in respect of want for I have
> learned, in whatsoever state I am, therewith
> to be content." (Philippians 4:11)

If you take your eyes off your surroundings, you can end up making your situation worse. The battle of uncontrolled thoughts starts within the mind. Do you know that the way you act stems from the way you feel? How you feel also determines the way you think. That's why the Bible tells us to think about the things that are of an excellent report (Philippians 4:8). Remember, the Holy Spirit lives inside you. He is Shalom; He is peace. God has called you and me to live a life of joy, abundance, and peace.

Activities for the caregiver can be as simple as reading, breathing exercises, and listening to relaxing music. Walking in the park can keep your mind alert, sharp, and focused. Remember, the Scripture tells us as a man thinketh in his heart, so is he (Proverbs 23:7). You must mentally learn to overcome your aversion to exercise. Think about it: Getting a pro-exercise mindset is not a sprint but a marathon. Start small and work your way up. Sprinting and marathons are in total opposition to each other, but they have common denominators: Both are challenging and consist of intense training. Sprinters' goal is short-term, while marathoners are in it for the long haul.

I recall being a sprinter in high school. In preparation for the city and state finals, the coach would set practice at another level. So one's training had to change to ensure the ability to compete with endurance; we were given workouts with the long-distance runners. Our team was ahead of the competition at a track meet, so the coach said to the sprinters, "I just entered you all in the distance race."

Our reaction was "What!" Now, we had practiced long-distance running before, but, on that day, I was not prepared. So, we all lined up, and the gun went off. I felt unstoppable as I ran at top speed, as if I was doing the 100-yard dash. Hitting the curve was a breeze but let me say this: When I came around to that last straightaway, out of nowhere, my legs stopped working. My legs felt like there were weights on them. I could feel myself wobbling and staggering, trying to make it to the finish line. In the beginning, I'd been on autopilot; but toward the end, I felt like I wanted to quit altogether. After I crossed the finishing line, the coach came over, patted me on the shoulder, and asked, "Are you alright?" He went on to say, "Good race. Now, walk it out. You've completed the run."

Yes, indeed, I had finished the race. But, as I lay on the field, assessing what I could have done differently, I found myself thinking. I thought about the little details that I had missed from previous training, like how to pace yourself when you are a distance runner. I even thought about the crazy mistake of starting full speed ahead. My struggle in the race brought to light the root problem. I'd gone into the distance race with the wrong mindset; I'd been caught up in the adrenaline of a sprinter and starting too fast had been a big mistake for the long run. I'd been nervous to find myself in a long-distance race when I was accustomed to short distances. Steve Maraboli says, "Once your mindset changes, everything on the outside will change along with it." Had I taken a moment and said to myself, "Okay, you are now shifting to long-distance running. Remember this is new, so start slow and pace yourself," I would not have ended up finishing the race with my body worn out and I wouldn't have struggled mentally to complete the race.

Committing to your care may be an adjustment but seeing and feeling the progress in how you pour yourself into others is something you will never regret. Fulfillment leaves the caregiver with satisfaction, knowing that they helped their loved one as best as they could. Without giving it much thought, a caregiver hits the floor, both feet flat and full speed ahead to assist their loved one. While your assistance renders support and comfort, it also can create a new level of weight. That's why, as caregivers, we must understand the cost to us and find contentment in the journey. Happiness is about being anxiety-free in your current position. As a caregiver, you learn new things every day. God called you to this role because He knew you could handle it. He called us to be of assistance in the situation, not to control the situation. God never gave us caregivers the office of mending, sheltering, and preserving as our job description; it was our character. He will equip us for the assignment at hand.

Life can feel overwhelming. As a caregiver, I felt it was my duty to keep up with the day-to-day demands. Keeping up with other commitments could become vital and present. There were so many things to recall, deadlines to meet, and obstacles to face. Each task required energy and attention; at times, it was quite daunting. I was in full throttle. One day, I sat looking at my to-do list for the week and the one for the month, and I could not find a blank spot on the calendar. The calendar started to look like a menu at the buffet line. It included appointments, religious affairs, and personal agendas. It was interesting how even things I enjoyed doing could render me speechless.

So, I lay prostrate before the Lord in complete silence as the tears rolled down my face. In solitude, I cried out, and calmness soon came over me. That moment was my breakthrough. I could feel that the weight had lifted. Finding fulfillment was trusting that God held the world in the palm of His hand and that He had complete control. I had to realize that something might not get done on that day and could be pushed to the next day, and I had to be okay with that. The laundry might need to wait until the next day, and the invitation might need to be declined this time around. With all that the caregiver did, it was easy to get caught up in thinking that it was all on you. You did the research; you set up the daily menu, scheduled the appointments, finalized the decision, etc. with a long to-do list. No wonder you thought you were in control.

You should learn how to delegate assignments. Find out from those in your support system what they are good at. If one likes groceries, give them your shopping list. If another is fond of kids, ask them to plan activities with your children while you're taking your loved one for a doctor's visit. When you give various tasks to different people, they do not mind helping; tell them how. Asking for help doesn't make you weak; it makes you wise! Waiting until you are tired to ask for help isn't good, but asking for help when you feel exhausted brings strength, and replenishes your time.

I am grateful for having such a devoted support team. After I came out of my "Thank you, I'm fine" mentality, there were more than enough people willing to help, as I stated in Chapter 1. So, enlist the help of others. Learn to communicate to others the different ways in which you need their help. In your communication, please do not assume they already know what you need. Be confident and make the request clearly and precisely. Super characters have superpowers; at times, we think we can do it all by ourselves. But there is more strength in having someone help you along the way. Wonder Woman had Wonder Girl, Batman had Robin, and you, my friend, have a family and or friends who are willing to help. Ask, but most importantly, your help is of the Lord. And His power, His name is above every name.

Spiritually, stress will pull you away from your relationship with the Lord like a train running off its tracks. Prayer is the key. Sometimes, it seems complicated to pray. But when you begin to override that earthly issue and become like the little caboose saying, "I think I can," then you can because you can do all things through Christ Jesus, so PUSH. Pray Until Something Happens.

Let worship be your driving force. We look to Jesus Christ and reflect on the fact that our God will never leave us. When you are in a place where you can't seem to find words of praise and adoration, open the Bible, and begin to read: Psalm 95 and Psalm 100 are good starting points. God's word is a constant reminder to us that He has not given us fear or worry. You cannot control the change that is going on around you, but you can always learn to change your response to the situation. God will use a complex problem to increase your faith. Your request is not too small for God to answer. Whatever that answer maybe, he will respond. You may not even understand the solution He gives because He tells us that our ways are not His ways and that neither are our thoughts. I am ever grateful for the change. As believers, we are to give thanks in everything, not for everything (1 Thessalonians 5:18). Being content and blessing His name in everything says a lot about our Father in heaven. When things are going well in your life, it's easy to be thankful, but a heart of gratitude becomes visible when you are in the fight for faith.

It is best if you establish balance in life. Write out what is of priority for you for the day and put your attention there as you care for your loved one—at the close of the day, reflect on what you could achieve for your loved one and yourself.

Going through life's challenges alone can leave one feeling isolated. We are all limited and fallible. So, I guess you are wondering, "What do I do now?" You change the way you think because the Bible tells us as a man thinketh in his heart, so is he. Getting support from a health professional, a clergy member, your spouse, a family member, or a friend is essential. Go to that person that you can trust and share with them the feelings and thoughts you have been experiencing.

When people ask how they can help, do you reply, "I'm okay"? Please take a tip from me: Don't be reluctant to ask for help or feel that you are a burden to them. The Bible tells us to think about the things that are of excellent report. Remember, the Holy Spirit lives inside you. He is Shalom; He is peace. God has called you and me to live a life of joy, abundance, and peace.

CHAPTER 7

THE EMOTIONS OF A CAREGIVER

> For thou art my rock and my fortress; therefore, for thy name's sake lead me, and guide me. Psalm 31:3 KJV

Do you know that emotional distress can occur when one is experiencing concurrent cancer or another bout of any illness or injury? As you walk in Christ Jesus, when you choose to care for others, there will be spiritual attacks as well. The enemy comes to steal, kill, and destroy. Therefore, the enemy wants you to feel alone and isolated when caring for your loved ones. The enemy will also try to convince you that you are totally selfish if you care for yourself. Processing your emotions is okay; but when your emotions turn into pity, self-doubt, and anger, that's a red flag. It should be a warning to you. Grab a notebook and start journaling your emotions, stop what you are doing and have a word of prayer!

Why do you feel the way you do? No matter what issue arrives at your gate (the gate of the caregiver), you should understand that the one receiving care did not wake up one day and decide, "I'm going to enlist you as my caregiver." Having to take care of someone with an illness or disability stirs up emotional thoughts, which can be complicated. One may experience days when they have an inner sense of fulfillment and a great connection with the other person. Then there are the not-so-happy days when one feels sad, guilty, or angry. There may even be times when your feelings begin to clash, for instance, you may have love and resentment at the same time. What makes you sad may not make the other person sad. There is no pill that the medical doctor can prescribe that will stop one from feeling the way they feel. One cannot tell the other that they should not feel a certain way. Emotions are part of the human makeup.

Many people can have various degrees of conflicting feelings at one time or another, and those feelings can arrive in different packages. They may range from being appreciative to being unappreciative and from being unconfined to being restricted. Some of you may even have lost your tempers or said things that you regret. At times, you may display less than super excited feelings about your role; emotions arise whether you want them to come forth or not. And at times, those feelings of anger, being on edge, and sadness make you feel guilty. I know that right now, as you read these words, you are saying, "Oh, that has never been me; I have never felt that way about anyone that I love. I could never (or would never) feel that way." For some, that has not always been the case. There are many people who are reluctant to talk about this. Continuously holding onto feelings and not talking through them can lead to headaches and discomfort. I know that your true intention is not to be on the other side; overall, you want peace to abide.

Here are a few examples. If your parent or loved one has been diagnosed with Alzheimer's, you spend your days recalling who you are to them and the importance of them taking their medication. That frustrates you, and there may even be moments when you feel heartbroken. You do not want to feel like you are selfish about the situation, so what do you do? You say, "Forget about what I'm feeling," and suppress it all. I say to you who is struggling with the way this illness has changed your loved one, be understanding. According to Matthew 25:40, "Whatever you did for one of the least of these brothers and sisters of mine, you did for me." Remember that it is love that "bears all things, believes all things, hopes all things and endures all things" (I Corinthians 13:7) that may come our way and that love is patient and is kind (I Corinthians 13:4). It is easier to let the little annoyances roll off; that will keep your heart and mind at peace.

If one parent is left alone, you may become their guardian and support. This can cause resentment in you, especially if other siblings are involved. You may wonder, "Why do I have to do this all by myself? Why isn't my sister or brother stepping in to help me out?" Reflect on 1 Timothy 5:4, which says, "But if any widow has children or nephews, let them learn first to shew piety at home, and to requite their parents: for that is good and acceptable before God." Every circumstance that God calls you to face is for you, and you cannot pass it to others.

Look at this as another way to show them the love and that they gave you from birth. Sometimes, while you are amid caring for your parent, they may be unkind to you in word or deed, and you may feel unappreciated. Take a moment, step back, and think, "How would I feel if that was me being limited or restricted?" Allow them to move as freely as possible and pray for them. Being your parent's support system is pleasing to God. Allow your parent to keep their independence as much as possible, allowing them to go and do within their limits what they can do. At the same time, show that you honor them by doing what you have been called to do for them. Pray for your siblings that they too may come to understand the support that is needed. Try setting up a family meeting and discussing the need and support you need from them.

Family members and siblings who do not live nearby are also called to care. If you are a long-distance caregiver, you can provide your loved one with support by way of check-ins by phone, have flowers or a fruit basket sent, give financial help, and pay a particular bill. However, also note that, if you are a long-distance caregiver, nothing can replace an in-person visit.

If your wife has given birth for the third time and there is still only one income in the house, you may be thinking, "Why didn't she plan better? I can't possibly do this all by myself." So you may begin to think to yourself that you have no capacity to take care of another child, and you may feel frustrated. And your wife may be sad. Try telling God how much you trust Him even if you feel like you don't. Ask Him to help you to rest and stand on His promises, for it is He, the Lord, who goes before you, and He will be with you and never fail or forsake you; therefore, be not afraid (Deuteronomy 31:8). Do not lean on what you think you know because God will show you the right thing to do: Seek His face.

If your spouse has been diagnosed with an illness and is facing the uncertainty of their standard of care, remind yourself that God is in control. He has seen the closing act. He knows the entire situation and is working out the purposes and plans for both of your lives. I say to you, take Him at His word and keep prayer as your lifeline. Stand on His word, including that which says that healing is the children's bread.

If you are taking care of a disabled child and looking for personal and supportive care for their daily activities, do you feeling guilty for asking "Why my child?" and worrying about the medical bills? You may realize that you can't take care of the child alone and need help from someone else, whether it's a family member or a professional caregiver or aide. Although that may be the best decision you have ever made for the both of you, you may feel inadequate at times, trust the process.

One of the hardest things in life is witnessing children suffering from illness or living with a disability. Do you recall the biblical story about a man who was born blind? The disciples saw Jesus paying attention to him, and they became concerned. They wanted to know whether it was the man or his parents who had sinned. So they were looking for Jesus to tell them whose fault it was. Well, neither was to blame. The answer didn't lie in blaming someone; it lay in Jesus's saying, *"It was not that this man sinned, or his parents, but that the works of God might be displayed in him"* (John 9:3). So the blindness was not about anyone's past sins but about showing what could be done to solve the issue.

Jesus was sent to destroy the works of the devil and heal the oppressed, so, in the midst of Jesus's works, God received the Glory. Given our various emotions, some irritation and confusion may arise as anger tries to find its place. Let me help ease your mind: Even the most compassionate person experiences frustration; it's part of the human package. Resentment can build up when there is no outlet for feeling hurt, sad, or angry. I want to share with you a connection that will help you. Look to Jesus at the very beginning of every circumstance, in the middle of the circumstance, and at its end. When you care for someone, you will lay aside your itinerary to focus on the hierarchy of importance: You will prioritize them. During care, when fear, anxiety, or frustration try to make an entry, the Christian in you should take it as a gentle reminder that you cannot make this journey all by yourself. You need the assistance of the Heavenly Father for His peace and understanding to reign over you. Look at David in the Bible; he began to pour out his heart to God when he was feeling very emotional. He gave it all to God, and God stepped in. At the end of the day, you, too, are a child of the Most High God. So, allow the Holy Spirit to come in and show you understanding. Next time you are experiencing emotional health challenges, look past your loved one's actions, which may tend to offend or hurt you. Those reactions are not about you, so give them grace as the Lord has extended it to you. Be grateful.

As believers, we are to give thanks in everything, not for everything. Being able to be content and bless His name in everything says a whole lot about our Father in heaven.

PRAYER

Heavenly Father, heal me from all physical, mental, emotional, and social discomfort. I know You want me to be happy, healthy, healed, and whole. I know You want me to live without anxiety, so I ask that You heal me, oh God, from all forms of regret and resentment. Help me to balance out my life, keeping You at the forefront, because, wherever You lead me, Lord, I will follow.

CHAPTER 8

THE STRENGTH OF A CAREGIVER

> "He giveth power to the faint; and to them that have
> no might he increaseth strength." (Isaiah 40:29)

"I don't know how you do this," is a phrase the caregiver hears often. If we are honest with ourselves, we don't understand how we do it either. We all have various gifts and talents. It is the gift of God that we caregivers can do what God has called us to do. It's all by His power. God is the way that makes all things possible.

It was in Gethsemane that Jesus gained strength. Jesus called on his three closest friends, Peter, James, and John, to watch while He prayed. Here, Jesus wrestled with the thought that He was about to be tortured and humiliated by man. Jesus cried out and asked His heavenly Father to get Him out of what He was about to face: the trial and crucifixion. We have all experienced wanting God to get us out of something. Maybe you wanted to hear a different report from the doctor. Jesus did not stop at the point of pain. He turned to the Father and said, "Nevertheless, let thy will be done." So go to God in prayer, for He already knows your problem. Jesus wants you to tell Him what you want.

Jesus became distraught, and He fell with His face to the ground. Praying on and off throughout the night, Jesus would periodically return to the three disciples and find them asleep. He began to say, "Can you not stay awake one hour?" Jesus did not let that frustrate him. He continued to go back, soliciting their prayers. Your inner circle may not be as readily available as you would like but keep each other posted on the outcomes of or adjustments to your prayers. Sharing how you feel with your spouse, family member, or close friend can make a difference. Jesus went away from the disciples a second time and prayed. He could see that the disciples were tired, so He went and prayed a third time as they slept. I say to you, do not stop praying, do not give up, go back, and pray again!

Jesus even asked the Father if that cup could be taken away so that He would not have to endure it. He ended his prayer with the words *"not my will, but thine, be done"* (Luke 22:42). The time had come for the soldiers to take Jesus away; Peter, James, and John arose. Undoubtedly, the Almighty God did not take the suffering away but gave Him strength to endure the cross. Know that when you are at your weakest point, the power of Jesus will rest on you.

According to Healthline.com, hematidrosis is a rare condition in which one begins to sweat blood. This happens when a person feels intense stress or fear. Someone facing death may feel such intensity. Typically, when a person is under stress, their body goes into fight or flight mode. In this case, the person's fight or flight mode ruptures the body's capillaries, especially around the sweat glands.

The mental and spiritual battle Jesus encountered in the garden was that tense. The Greek word "thrombose" is a medical term used to describe thick blood. The Bible says that Jesus's thick blood drops fell to the ground. The worst-case scenario that you have encountered does not begin to compare to the combat Jesus endured. The disciples were human. They could not stay awake. Do you recall a time when Jesus was calling you to commune with Him, yet you were tired? There were times when I set my alarm so that I could rise early in the morning and spend time in prayer and devotion, but given the sleepless night before, my physical body was weak. My spirit was willing, though. Recognize that fatigue is on the rise and that it will negatively affect you.

The Bible tells you to call upon Him, and He will show you things you do not know (Jeremiah 33:3). Honestly, there are things in life that we do not understand. On top of your daily routine, if you have no plan, you are setting yourself up for disruption. So, before you start the day, make sure to put in your time with the Lord first. Spending time with the Lord will redirect your thoughts and actions. It's not always the number of hours that matters, so pay attention to the quality of your intentions. Make time with the Father. We are created to need Him! Consult the

Holy Spirit in your choices throughout the day to guide you as you care for your loved one.

Overall, put your trust in Christ for whatever situation you may experience. Jesus, who was sinless, did the will of the Father because of His love for humanity. As a caregiver, you also have the compassion and love to help others. Galatians 6 tells us to encourage our sister or brother when they faced struggles. You may not get all the answers to your prayers you want. He will give you the courage and tenacity to go through.

Naturally, we too often want to treat the symptoms and not the cause. Tending to divide or categorize the issues will affect us mentally, physically, and spiritually. God allowed me to see myself after I engaged in much prayer and fasting, and I realized that I could not be a perfect caregiver. It's ok if you don't catch every symptom that your loved one has; it's ok that you fell asleep while your loved one was receiving a treatment. God is the one who is all-knowing and all-powerful. Stop second-guessing yourself. Remember, caregivers, you will not be able to handle everything occurring in your loved ones' lives. Instead, do your portion, and let Him do the rest!

PRAYER

Heavenly Father, as I lay before you, hear my cry, oh Lord. I ask for forgiveness for thinking wrong of myself and others. I command every spirit of fear and negative pressure to leave my mind, body, and confidence in Jesus's name. My mind is focused on pure and lovely things.

I come to you, Lord, to share that, at times, when I feel discouraged, weak, and worried, you are there to comfort me by way of a phone call as someone asks what is needed or a knock at the door as someone just stops by to see if they could be of assistance. Please help me to reply, "Yes!" I know you want me to live free of anxiety, fear, stress, and worry. Help me to find rest in you, oh Lord!

CHAPTER 9

THE RESTORATION OF A CAREGIVER

> "Come unto me, all ye that labor and are heavy
> laden, and I will give you rest." (Matthew 11:28)

As a caregiver, it's necessary to take the time to fulfill your essential obligations such as eating, resting, exercising, and even taking supplements. Refilling your cup allows you to refresh and pour yourself into others. Through the eyes of the Creator, we have been made wonderfully and marvelously. Proverbs 19:8 states, "He that getteth wisdom loveth his own soul: he that keepeth understanding shall find good." Your self-care is important not just for you but also for others. You can't function well if you are not well.

I recall sitting in an airplane. In preparation for the takeoff, the flight attendant announced the safety briefing. The flight attendant said that in the event of an emergency, if decompression occurred, we had to make sure our masks were on before helping others. So, in the event of the call to care, make sure you have your mask on first; you don't want to run out of oxygen by feeling burned out and exhausted. You also run the risk of becoming ill yourself, which will not benefit anyone else. Oxygen is your first and greatest source of energy. Without oxygen, the brain cells die and deteriorate quickly. Experiencing brain fog will keep you off your A-game. If you are unable to take care of yourself, how will you be able to take care of others who need your support? Self-care involves taking action to improve your health. It's an activity that you should do deliberately to take care of yourself mentally, physically, spiritually, and emotionally. Are you thriving in life or just living? Living life and feeling overwhelmed is not the way our God intended us to live. The word of God says, *"For I know the plans I have for you,' declares the LORD, 'plans to prosper you and not to harm you, plans to give you hope and a future'"* (Jeremiah 29:11). Therefore, God does not want us to live lives in which we are bound mentally, physically, and emotionally.

When God says in the Scripture that all things work together for our good, his definition of "good" is not the same as ours. To the Israelites, God made a promise that, one day, they would soon go back home. He reminded them that He would never leave them, so they had to put their faith in His word while they were going through hardship. God can see much further than we can. We can see the hill and imagine in our minds that it will be a long journey to get to the top. So, while we are trying to figure out how long it will take us to go up the hill, Jesus has already done it and is on the other side. On that side, Jesus is saying, "You have made it, you have won the victory." Although you can't see what is on the other side of the mountain, know that Jesus has made the journey for you.

Physical care entails how you are keeping up with maintenance in your body. Think about it this way: Routine maintenance on your car is necessary. It can seem like a waste of time and unnecessary, but what happens when you fail to keep the maintenance up? You face more repairs, possible accidents, and major breakdowns, along with an unexpected, very expensive bill. Without maintenance, you decrease the lifespan of the vehicle. You see, it's the little things like oil changes and fluids being refueled and flushed that can prevent you from experiencing heart failure—sorry, I mean engine failure.

Paul tells us in Ephesians 5:29, *"No one ever hated his own flesh, but nourishes and cherishes it."* Initially, it's those small issues that can lead to lifelong irreversible damage. How often do you get a checkup at the doctor's office? Routine checkups and exams with your primary doctor are important. Keep track of your test results so that, when you see the doctor, you have a reference to go back to. Know the signs and symptoms of what is going on in your body so that the doctor can prescribe the correct medication instead of providing a general protocol until something else shows up that may indicate another direction to take. The doctor needs to know the truth about how you are feeling and what is going on, so do not omit the small details; this will help the doctor prescribe a more accurate treatment for your condition. You only get one physical body, so take charge!

In the Scriptures, Paul tells us to present our bodies as a living sacrifice (Romans 12:1), so we should present our bodies as worship unto Him. You cannot go out witnessing to others and compelling them to turn to Christ when your body is in pain.

How much sleep are you really getting? Adults need, on average, at least 7–8 hours of sleep at night. Sleep calms your body down. Proper sleep yields you better concentration for the next day and allows you to make wiser choices. How much physical activity do you participate in? Exercise increases the endorphins within your body that cause you to feel better from the inside out. Walking just thirty minutes a day will improve your day and can help you get a better night's rest. When you find yourself tired on a regular basis, you cannot do some of the things that a Christian should do, for instance, rising early in the morning to pray.

How are you eating? Are you just getting by on carbs and sugary drinks throughout the day? Occasionally enjoying sugary items is not a bad thing, but continuously eating them can lead to many health issues. Limit their intake and enjoy them in moderation. Think about the rainbow God put in the sky; it is colorful and beautiful to look at. The more colorful your fruits and vegetables are (in addition to the vitamins and minerals they provide), the healthier you are. Eating foods that are nutritious is very important. Staying hydrated by drinking water and eating well allows you to feel better, and you can lower your risk of heart disease and speed up your healing process. Start off by making small changes to your eating habits; try adding one new healthy item to what you eat. While attending to your loved one, make sure you eat several meals a day so that you have the energy to serve.

Are you exercising? Exercise will alleviate your stress, boost your mood, and increase your energy level, reducing inflammation throughout your body and enhancing your heart health. All activity counts, believe it or not; exercise can be done almost anywhere and anytime. Those that have a fixed mindset when it comes to exercise may feel that there is nothing, they can do to conquer the thought of that dreadful word "exercise." Instead, they should think of it in terms of "movement time." Your body will indicate to you when it needs to be stretched; just listen. How often do you find tension in parts of your body and remain uncomfortable until you move? Stretch even if it's just leaning your head from side to side and then forward and backward. At times, you may have a cramp in your calf. What do you do? You stand and begin to stretch. Stretching increases the blood flow to the muscles within your body. If you don't remember to exercise or feel that there isn't enough time to do a forty-five-minute workout, take advantage of the times when you are watching TV. During commercial breaks, get up and stretch. Living in a digital world, you can easily find an exercise app that will remind you it's time to get up and move!

Laughter burns calories. Proverbs 17:22 in the New Living Translation says, *"A cheerful heart is a good medicine, but a broken spirit saps a person's strength."* Laughter is good for the soul. Laughter is contagious; surround yourself with those who have a sense of humor and make you laugh. According to the Mayo Clinic, stress is relieved by laughter. Look for opportunities to laugh out loud. Laughter can help your body heal, boosting your immune system and decreasing your stress hormones. Build enough time so that optimal time is created and enjoyed."

CHAPTER 10

THE PEACE OF A CAREGIVER

> "Now the Lord of peace himself give you peace always by all means. The Lord be with you all." (2 Thessalonians 3:16)

God never promised that we would give ourselves Peace. As a caregiver, on many days, you will need the Peace of God. We are always trying to produce Peace in our homes, workplaces, circumstances, and minds, only to find ourselves feeling unsettled. True Peace is not found in man or in your community. In the midst of the care recipients' adverse reactions, abnormal test results, visits to the emergency room, and consultations, you will find a place of rest through Peace. Not until you exercise your faith will you obtain Peace. Nourishing your spirit is essential.

Prayer is an effective way to grow in your faith. For faith comes by hearing, and hearing comes by way of the word of the Lord.

Faith requires you to do something as a caregiver. God tells us to praise Him in the middle of our circumstances. One thing is for sure: God is a sovereign God, and He always hears me. I John 5:14 tells us, "This is the confidence that we have in him, that if we ask anything in his name, he heareth us." We must work at listening to the instructions. Hold onto your faith. Know that your level of prayer may change, but the one who hears your prayer changes not. God always keeps His promises.

John 3:16 beautifully tells us how much God loves us and that we can participate in a life of eternity. Prayer should be a daily routine; your prayer life needs to be a daily habit. Sickness and disease make it challenging to find Peace. Mirror what you do in nature; just as you wash your face to rid it of dirt, the washing of the word by water is essential. God does not work apart from his word. Wash and come alive in the rivers of living water. A person with a healthy, happy soul is alive in Jesus Christ. So let the waters spring forth, bringing healing words from you; out of your belly will flow blessings for support and encouragement to others. God will grant you Peace when you cast all your concerns unto Him. God's Grace is keeping me.

The soul is the very essence of who we are: *"The Lord God formed man of the dust of the ground, and breathed into his nostrils the breath of life; and man became a living soul"* (Genesis. 1:7). To incorporate all aspects of our being is to rise and bless the Lord as Psalm 103 tells us. You are a marvelous work in His eyes. You are a soul that is housed in a body here on earth. Are your body, mind, and soul unified? When your soul and body are not well, you are misaligned, and that causes a disruption to your health that we call disease.

Let's turn to the book of 1 Kings 19:8, bible story of Elijah, who needed to devote attention to both his self-care and soul care. Elijah began to flee for his life after Jezebel heard that he had defeated the prophets of Baal.

While hiding in the cave, he became frustrated and was physically tired. Elijah had become distraught to the extent that he'd wanted to go to the cave in mount Carmel land not go on. God showed His love towards him by providing food, rest and time for him to replenish, restore, and rejuvenate himself within those forty days. Our souls need restoration.

Soul care involves taking care of the whole person: mind, body, and soul. Living an abundant life is not the same as your life being on autopilot. Feeling disengaged, depleted, and depressed is not living a great life. If you don't get proper rest at night, you cannot rise early to seek the Lord.

Yes, I needed self-care for my physical, mental, emotional, and social support, but it was the soul care from the Father that drew me closer and allowed me the time and space to commune with Him. My soul communicates with my spirit. The space that I created was intentional: to love my neighbor as myself, to live and lead well.

Your soul should be anchored in the Lord because, if you do not make a habit of being quiet before the Lord, you will forget who God is and all the many blessings and benefits that He wants to share with you. You may not be able to change the course of the loved one that you are caring for but know that God is intentionally changing you to be more like Him in the process. It's all for His Glory! C.S. Lewis states, "Relying on God has to begin every day as if nothing had yet been done."

The law of the Lord is perfect, converting the soul: The testimony of the Lord is sure, making wise the simple. Spending quality time with the Father will allow you to live out His purpose here on earth.

In soul care, you take time to glean something from the inner voice that says, "When you are weak, I am strong": "My soul longeth, even fainteth for the courts of the Lord: my heart and my flesh crieth out for the Living God" (Psalm 84:2).

Your soul should be anchored in the Lord because, if you do not make a habit of being quiet before the Lord, you will forget who God is and all the many blessings and benefits that He wants to share with you. You may not be able to change the course of the loved one that you are caring for but know that God is intentionally changing you to be more like Him in the process. It's all for His Glory!

CONCLUSION

As a caregiver, I want to share with you and encourage you: You are not alone. He will fight for you! God is in your corner. He will send you help and resources.

It's important for you to be healthy and watch out for the warning signs so that you do not lose yourself while taking care of others; make sure that you put your mask on first. Now, at any time, you can be called on to care for someone. Whatever the situation you are facing, know that it was predetermined. The Fight is fixed. Jesus won your Fight on the cross over 2021 years ago, and in the midst of the various blows He took for you and me, you now have the victory.

Remember the F.I.G.H.T. Faith in God Holds True against any and all circumstances, sickness, or disease. Trust in God; he will carry you through.

Be encouraged if you are reading this now and are going through a fiery trial or test with a loved one who was given a report of cancer or any sickness. The Bible confirms in James 5:14–15, "Is anyone among you sick? Let him call for the elders of the church, and let them pray over him, anointing him with oil in the name of the Lord, and the prayer of faith will save the sick, and the Lord will raise him up. And if he has committed sins, he will be forgiven." Ask the person with the sickness to confess their sins, and, in your daily prayer time, include the following:

- Worship music
- Healing Scriptures
- Decreeing and declaring that the assignment of sickness is canceled
- Speaking and commanding the sickness to leave
- Declaring that the symptom you see will leave
- Commanding every part of the body to line up with the word of God and declaring that the body parts will function in the perfection God created them to function in
- Commanding the cancer cells not to multiply
- Commanding the radiation not to affect the good (healthy) cells
- Cursing the cancer cells so that they may be destroyed and leave the body, and commanding that they not come near the healthy cells as they exit
- Commanding the body not to reject the chemotherapy or the prescribed medications
- When a loved one is nauseous from medical treatment, commanding the stomach to keep the food taken down

- Declaring that the spirit of fear will not come near your loved one's presence
- Commanding every negative person's mouth to be shut
- Declaring that the will of God be done on earth as it is in heaven
- Calling on Jehovah–Shalom; for He is peace: "Call Him, and He will answer" (Jeremiah 33:3).

F — Faith

I — In

G — God

H — Holds

T — True

Prayer of Salvation

If you are a non-Christian caregiver and you find yourself alone, I want you to take a moment and ask the Father to be in your corner. Would you mind praying this prayer with me?

I am a sinner in need of a savior. The word of God says that all have sinned and fallen short of the Glory of God (Romans 3:23). So I now repent and yield my life to You. Forgive me for my sins; You said in Your word that if I confessed with my mouth the Lord Jesus and believed in my heart that God raised Him from the dead, I was saved.

WELCOME TO THE BODY OF CHRIST!

You have made a major step, and guess what? You are not alone! God is glad that you have accepted HIM, and I accept you too! Please feel free to contact me and share how God has given you the grace to care for someone. Be Blessed!

Appendix A:
Self-Care Tips

John 15

1. **Prayer** – It is your lifeline, your Home Depot. This is the route through which you can enter the presence of God. According to Luke 18:1, "And he spake a parable unto them to this end, that men ought always to pray, and not to faint." Seek the Father, and do His will.

2. **Expectations** – Hold fast to the word of God. He wants you to make Him a priority. He expects you to talk to Him about your needs.

3. **Meditation** – Think about the promises of God, for the promises of God are "Yes" and "Amen." Read the Scriptures; memorize the Scriptures.

4. **Rest** – Spend quality time with the Father so that you can be strengthened and your faith may develop. Take a moment to engage in activities that help you enjoy life.

APPENDIX B:
RESOURCES AND REFERENCES

Support groups are available in most areas. Try doing an internet search or ask your primary physician and local church.

AARP (American Association of Retired Persons)

American Cancer Society : https://www.cancer.org/treatment/ treatments-and-side-effects/treatment-types/surgery/ ostomies/ileostomy/what-is-ileostomy.html

https://companionsforseniors.com/2020/04/patience -empathy-compassion-caregivers/

https://www.biblegateway.com/KJV

https://www.blessedbutstressed.com/2013/08/06/definition -of-a-caregiver-you/

https://www.caregiving.org/

https://www.christiancaregiversupport.com/

https://www.comfortkeepers.com/

https://www.rosalynncarter.org/about-us/

https://www.healthline.com/health/hematidrosis

National Institute of Mental Health -- https://www.nimh.nih.gov/health/publications/depression-in-women

QUOTE BY DR. MARTIN LUTHER KING, JR.

https://www.selfhelpdaily.com/quotes-by-martin-luther-king-jr/

Helping Yourself Help Others: A Book for Caregivers (Paperback) – December 26, 1995, by Rosalynn Carter.

....

For more information or to contact

Lisa F. Harris

✉ ladylisaharris@gmail.com

....

www.ingramcontent.com/pod-product-compliance
Lightning Source LLC
Chambersburg PA
CBHW071144090426
42736CB00012B/2221